PROMISES KEPT

*Industry Legends Share How People of Character Keep
Promises Through the Miracle of Life Insurance*

Edward G. Deutschlander, CLU®, CLF®
P. Shaun McDuffee, CLU®, ChFC®, AEP®, CEPA®
Phillip C. Richards, CFP®, CLU®, RHU®

ISBN 13: 978-0-578-18775-4

DEDICATION

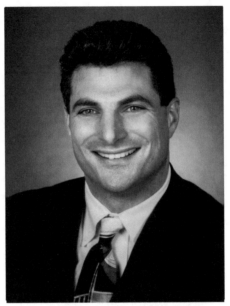

Scott H. Richards, CLU, ChFC
1962–2008

Life insurance is a miracle product that ensures financial security for families when their primary income earner dies. Those financial advisors who realize that life insurance—risk protection—should anchor every financial plan are truly "Miracle Merchants." And those people of character who truly love their families *show* their love by securing life insurance long before they think they might need it.

No one has conveyed the truth of this message as eloquently or passionately as Scott Richards. Scott, the firstborn son of Phil Richards, one of this book's authors, lost his courageous six-year battle with myelofibrosis and acute myeloid leukemia on July 12, 2008. Two years before he died at age forty-five, early in 2006, Scott spoke from the main platform at GAMA International's LAMP conference. Here is what he said:

> One of the blessings that has come from my medical condition was the realization that living a long life no longer was a sure thing, and it isn't for any of those you serve, either. It has not only given me a firsthand experience with the emotions our clients endure, but it has allowed me the relief of knowing their families will be taken care of financially due to the Miracle of Life Insurance. Also, I can now look another person in the eye and tell them death is a guarantee. Not even my compliance department or the regulators can prevent me from guaranteeing this truth—but they did hold it up for about three months while they discussed it! We need to prepare for it and help others to do the same.

It has been said that there are no atheists in foxholes, and I believe there are even fewer in hospital beds.

It was not until death was real and imminent that my faith was tested. During this time, Michelle and I were strengthened by our belief in knowing where I would ultimately go. Winston Churchill said, "I'm ready to meet my maker. Whether my maker is prepared for the ordeal of meeting me is another matter." Fortunately for now, I remain on the right side of the sod, and in my case, my physician thinks that I will have the gift—and believe me, it is a gift—of at least ten more years of life. I am resolved to make this gift count for something that really matters, and every one of you and those you serve really and truly matter. I pray that each of you will do the same. Fortunately, we are in this great business that gives us the opportunity to change lives in profound ways.

My health issue has definitely ignited a passion to use whatever remaining time I have left to do what I can to build our industry for others. I hope you make your life be the spark that ignites your agency and company because each passing day becomes more precious and is an investment in our values and in the very purpose of our being. It is not only important to have these values, but it is just as important to express them with those we care about. Writing letters, which remain with my insurance policies, to Michelle and Lauren that express my love for them, was one of the hardest things I have ever had to do. Knowing that this would be the last chance I would have to say, "I love you" in this life was extremely difficult.

I am sharing this with you because if you will do this for your family, it will change your very outlook on this business. These letters *tell* them how much I love them, but my life insurance really *shows* them that love.

ℰ◯ℭℛ

As you can see, Scott's illness didn't depress him; instead, it energized him. It not only gave him a sense of purpose but added urgency to that purpose, since he could see the end from where he was, but now he saw the miracle, up close and personal. He witnessed firsthand the peace of mind and the serenity that come from knowing that your loved ones are out of harm's way, out of danger, safe. He could see clearly that his vision was in perfect focus. He was living the very miracle he had been preaching and teaching about. Because of life insurance, Scott's vision was not a nightmare but instead would prove to be the fulfillment of a beautiful dream. He said often to anyone who appeared sad about his condition, "Don't feel bad. Either way, I win. If I die, I get to spend eternity with my Lord and Savior. If I live, I get to walk down the aisle and give my precious daughter, Lauren, away in marriage. But either way, I win."

> **Life is not about duration but about donation.**

Scott believed that life was not measured by its length, but by its breadth. Life is not about duration but about donation. At no point during those horrific six years of intermittent chemotherapy, numerous punishing bone marrow biopsies, and long hospital stays was Scott ever scared. His condition, courage, and clarity of vision were contagious, and they energized all around him. He received more than 34,000 messages of love and encouragement on his Caring Bridge website. We were all grateful for the support.

His bravery was an inspiration to all of us. On February 29, 2008, five months before he died, Scott wrote in his diary,

"Courage is not absence of fear, but the belief that there is something more important than our fear. Love of others, family, will conquer fear every time."

Scott may have been in the gutter, but he was looking up at the stars. During his last months, life insurance allowed him to look at things philosophically rather than worry about the well-being of his family if the worst were to happen. As Life Happens says, life insurance is not for the dead but for the living. And in this case, that included Scott himself.

The Mayo Clinic doctors told Scott that he could expect to live at least ten years, which would give him time to enjoy his children growing up, time to enjoy quality time with his wife, Michelle, and time to mentor more agents. As you know, this life is unpredictable, and in Scott's case it was. When our family feared the worst, we decided to bring Lauren and Nicholas, ages six and three, into the intensive care unit at Mayo to see their father, maybe for the last time. On July 12, 2008, minutes after the children left his room, Scott died. Breathing on a respirator, he held on for those final minutes to see Lauren and Nick one last time.

The best doctors in the world can be wrong. The medical evidence can be wrong. Statistics can be wrong. In the final analysis, nothing in this life is guaranteed. The best doctors in the world, shocked at Scott's passing, couldn't save him. His strength, his courage, and his extreme will couldn't extend his life. But the one thing that Scott counted on was his life insurance, and it wasn't wrong. It could, and it did, help him, as well as his cherished loved ones. It made all the difference. Scott's life insurance was his permission slip to live life at its fullest, serving and mentoring others in spite of his condition.

When people of character buy life insurance, they are keeping a promise to secure their loved ones' financial future.

And when courageous financial advisors who believe in the Miracle of Life Insurance provide it, they are keeping a promise to their clients to remove their worries about their families' financial future.

Today and every day, life insurance is still showing Scott's wife, Michelle, and their two children, Lauren and Nick, how much Scott loved them. Lauren and Nick have a full-time mom, still live in their same home, attend their same private schools, and live in their same neighborhood with their same friends with plenty of worry-free time to love one another and without any worry about their college education or their financial future. Short of a physical presence, Scott, through his life insurance, is there with them in every other way, every day.

"When he lived, he lived for you. Now that he is gone, he lives in you."

As poet John Donne said, "Death be not proud." While death didn't intend it, its deed freed Scott of his tortured body and delivered him into the loving arms of his Creator. Scott did not live or die in vain. His legacy lives on in everyone he mentored and touched. His legacy lives on in every one of you who sells the miracle. The Chinese say it like this: "When he lived, he lived for you. Now that he is gone, he lives in you." Scott's perfect vision lives on in every one of you who believes in the Miracle of Life Insurance. Scott knew that the only takeaways from this life are those things we have given away. The testimonies to purposeful lives, the sharing, the caring, the love, the wisdom of good thoughts, and the comforts of life to loved ones if our lives are cut short are made possible through the Miracle of Life Insurance.

Like Scott, financial advisors who recognize the importance of life insurance are the mentors and the Miracle Merchants who allow primary income earners to keep promises to their families.

If you are a financial advisor who is committed to ensuring families' financial protection through life insurance, we honor you. If you are a primary income earner for your family, we urge you to secure life insurance for your family today. In doing so, you will demonstrate your love for them like nothing else ever could. If you have already done so, you are a person of character who has taken the biggest step possible toward securing your family's financial future in the event of your death.

ABOUT SCOTT'S CAREER

Scott Richards, CLU, ChFC, entered the financial services industry in 1984 and enjoyed a successful career as a financial advisor to business owners and other affluent individuals. In 1994, Scott joined the North Star Management Team as Vice President of North Star Resource Group. Scott's key roles involved sales and marketing initiatives, as well as leading North Star's Business-to-Business Marketing and Advisor Recognition Programs. He was a member of the International Association of Financial Planners (IAFP) and the National Association of Insurance and Financial Advisors (NAIFA), and he was president-elect of GAMA International's Minneapolis chapter.

Scott graduated with a bachelor of arts degree from the University of Minnesota, where he played for the Golden Gopher Varsity Football team. Scott and his wife, Michelle, were involved with various charitable organizations, such as Feeding Children International with their children, Lauren and Nicolas.

Scott lost a long and valiant battle with myelofibrosis and acute myeloid leukemia in 2008, but his legacy is carried on as a result of his philanthropy and compassion for others, as well as his lasting influence within the financial industry. Following his death, North Star Resource Group renamed its foundation the Scott Richards North Star Charitable Foundation and continues to honor Scott's legacy today.

ABOUT THE SCOTT RICHARDS NORTH STAR CHARITABLE FOUNDATION

In 2004, North Star established our own foundation to maximize our charitable contributions. Based on personal experiences the North Star family has had, we chose six causes as the focus of our foundation: ataxia, Alzheimer's disease, Bikes for Kids, breast cancer, cystic fibrosis, and myelofibrosis. In addition to strategic giving for these six diseases, North Star is committed to recognizing and supporting our own employees' volunteerism and charitable donations through an internal matching-funds program. North Star has made a commitment to donate 10 percent of its profits to the foundation. In the ten years leading to the writing of this book, the foundation has donated in excess of $3 million.

TABLE OF CONTENTS

SECTION 2
The Value of Life Insurance: Insight from the Industry's
Most Highly Respected Leaders

IMAGINE IF LIFE INSURANCE DIDN'T EXIST

Life insurance is a miraculous product. Buying life insurance is the ultimate demonstration of love a primary income earner can show his or her family. No one likes to face or talk about their mortality, but it is a fact of life. Those people who have the foresight and integrity to secure their families' future by buying life insurance are wise beyond measure. And those financial advisors who have the courage to bring up this difficult subject and urge their clients to get life insurance in place are honorable beyond measure. You are Miracle Merchants.

Life insurance is a promise kept.

The promise is that if you purchase life insurance and then die, your family members will receive money to help them avoid financial difficulties. Upon the death of an income earner who has life insurance in place, a financial advisor delivers a check to the beneficiaries, keeping the promise that was made the moment the life insurance policy went into effect.

WHY WE WROTE THIS BOOK

We wrote this book to remind every financial advisor and planner of his or her responsibility to place the proper amount of life insurance with clients and to invigorate them to commit to this important work. It is our hope that field leaders, home office leaders, and manufacturers also will commit to this work and spread this critical message.

We also want to urge any consumers who have not purchased a sufficient amount of life insurance to do so. When you buy life insurance, you are making a promise to your family that if you die unexpectedly, they will be taken care of financially. Make and keep this promise to them. And do it before you think you might need it. If you wait until you find out you have a medical condition, you most likely will be uninsurable. If you have already done so, we applaud this great decision you have made. You can have peace of mind and security because you have taken a step that will allow your family to live the life they want to live. And that will allow you to leave the legacy you envision.

The book was written by one of the industry's prominent advisors who has personal experience in this area (Shaun McDuffee) and two of the industry's prominent leadership executives (Phil Richards and Ed Deutschlander). We want this book to remind agents and advisors that it is our moral obligation to make people aware of the danger of being uninsured or underinsured. We want to impress upon everyone in this industry, and the general public, how critical it is to have sufficient

> **It is our moral obligation to make people aware of the danger of being uninsured or underinsured.**

life insurance in place. North Star Resource Group has more than $35 billion of life insurance in force, helping families nationwide achieve financial security upon the death of their primary income earners.

But what if life insurance didn't exist? Imagine that for a moment. If there were no such thing as life insurance, then when a family's primary income earner died, that family would have to rely on just their savings and the widow or widower's future earnings to sustain their current lifestyle. That is what people who have no life insurance do.

But thankfully, we do have life insurance. It is one of the most beneficial financial products ever created—but one of the most underused and least understood products. When a family's primary income earner dies unexpectedly, he or she was wise enough to secure life insurance previously, and the policy remains in force, then a check will be delivered to the family that will make it easier to continue living their current lifestyle. Life insurance is meant to be a source of comfort and peace of mind at a point in one's life that is stressful and filled with uncertainty.

Without life insurance, a family who loses the primary income earner to an untimely death is destined for hardship. The real tragedy is that this type of hardship is completely preventable.

This book contains true stories of families our company, North Star Resource Group, sold life insurance to and then delivered death benefits to when the primary income earner died. Those checks allow families to have hope for a more comfortable future. They can send their children to good schools and remain in their homes, and stay-at-home moms might not have to work outside the home. The book also contains the illuminating stories of eighteen high-level leaders in the insurance and financial services industry who believe in the Miracle of Life Insurance and believe it should be the anchor of every financial plan.

Decades ago, life insurance was our industry's main focus. In fact, it was our only focus. Then other financial products slowly began to push life insurance out of the equation. Many companies no longer sell life insurance at all. We believe this is a tragedy. No financial plan is complete without life insurance. Risk management should be the first financial concern agents and advisors address with their clients and prospective clients. It's not optional.

DO THE RIGHT THING

Yes, it is a difficult discussion. People don't like to think about, or talk about, their mortality. For that reason, most agents and advisors don't like to discuss life insurance with their clients. But we have a calling. By failing to offer life insurance to our clients,

40%
Americans without life insurance

we are putting families in harm's way. It is our obligation to talk to clients about what happens if they don't have life insurance—and what happens if they do. More than 40 percent of Americans have no life insurance, according to the 2015 Insurance Barometer Study by Life Happens and LIMRA.[1] That is a tragedy that is entirely preventable.

Back when most families typically had only one income earner, it was absolutely devastating when that person died,

1. "2015 Insurance Barometer Study," Life Happens website, https://www.lifehappens.org/industry-resources/agent/barometer2015/.

especially if it happened unexpectedly. That family was out on the street if the income earner died without having secured life insurance. Today, though, many families have dual incomes. So if something happens to one of the income earners, the family is not affected quite as much. Certainly they will have a drastic lifestyle change, but they are probably not going to be homeless; someone in the family is still earning an income. But in some cases, that fact has resulted in a decline in the number of families who own

> People say they will get by, but when reality hits them in the face, they are unprepared.

life insurance. It has added more denial to the situation. People think that if worst comes to worst, both parents are working, so they will get by. People say they will get by, but when reality hits them in the face, they are unprepared. And simply by purchasing life insurance, they could have had peace of mind, knowing that if something happened to one or both income earners, the remaining family members would have a secure financial future.

When I (Phil) was twenty-two years old, I met with a CPA in Philadelphia who was just two years older than me. He and his wife both came from poor backgrounds, and they had three young children. He applied for life insurance with Penn Mutual but was declined because he had a disease he never knew he had. He said to me, "What will I do? I had my hopes and dreams of getting this policy to take care of my family. You convinced me of the need for it, I agreed, and I did the health exam and everything you asked me to do, but I didn't get life insurance. I am uninsurable now. What do I do now?"

Imagine what he felt like. Imagine what I, a new life insurance agent, felt like.

Millions of people are walking around without knowing the risk they are running by failing to secure life insurance. They love their families but have not taken the one step they need to take to protect their loved ones' financial future. As a financial advisor, you are the keeper of this knowledge. You might be the only person who will ever spark the thought in a client's mind that he or she needs life insurance. What are you doing about it?

> If your true mission is to serve others and to help them be good stewards of their financial future, how could you possibly leave life insurance out of the equation?

When financial advising and financial planning professionals offer investment products but fail to address clients' risk management, they are leaving their souls behind, and they don't even realize it.

Taking advantage of the Miracle of Life Insurance is the right thing to do. For income earners, it's the right thing to do for their families. For advisors, it's the right thing to do for our clients.

BELIEVE IN MIRACLES

"Do you believe in miracles?" American television sportscaster Al Michaels posed this question as the final seconds ticked off the clock while the 1980 USA Olympic hockey team defeated the Soviet Union in perhaps the greatest sports upset of all time. It is one of the greatest questions to contemplate.

Believing in miracles is hope at its finest hour. It is, to a degree, accepting that things perhaps do happen for a reason, regardless of whether or not those reasons are ever revealed to us in our lifetime.

In our collective one-hundred-plus years of building advisors and serving clients, we have observed that the public often sees financial advisors as having an ability to see the future in somewhat of a "crystal ball." They expect financial advisors to make up for the time they have lost in not saving enough money, trying to time the market, and many other "sins" that are so easy to make when trying to "do it yourself."

So, along comes the "knight in shining armor," the financial advisor who can supposedly cure these ills and promise and guarantee that people will never outlive their money and that when the uncertainties of life occur (and indeed they will—none of us is immune), all will be fine. Many expect us to be *miracle workers*.

We must be the bearer of bad news. We are not miracle workers. The women and men who dedicate their life's work to being advisors are indeed a special breed. However, to expect us to perform miracles is not what any of us signed up for. What we did sign up for is to have a career—a calling, if you will—that is purpose- and values-driven and that ultimately makes a difference in people's lives. Within our firm, we have deemed this undertaking "Changing lives, forever." That is the inspiration, motivation, and drive behind every advisor—to somehow be able to educate, motivate, and inspire people to take action for their financial future and to be there to make sure they start and stay the course of this potentially turbulent journey to financial security.

> Society places expectations on us to be fortune tellers regarding how the market will perform on an hourly and daily basis. But we are not *miracle workers*; we are indeed *miracle merchants*.

The good news is that there is a specially trained team of values-driven people who have taken an oath to do whatever they can to ensure that the many values-driven people of character in this world are prepared for the inevitable and that they leave this world with dignity and a manner in which their loved ones will remember them for what they did do, not for what they didn't do. What they *did* do is leave a legacy, a permanent reminder that their families were loved—not only in words, but in deeds. Their selfless act of purchasing life insurance long before they thought they might need it will allow spouses, partners, children, grandchildren, business partners, employees, and communities to be able to say, "While this person was alive, he lived for us, and now he lives in us and will never be forgotten."

How does this happen? It happens with the miracle product of life insurance. That is what this book is dedicated to—the financial advisors who are indeed what their title claims: financial advisor. The purest of the financial advisors have an upbringing, indoctrination, and appreciation for this miraculous product. Sure, they also have expertise in other areas and work with securities, retirement, education, and estate-planning products. But the very best have been trained on life insurance, have a sense of pride in it, and more importantly, have a sense of obligation and responsibility to do something very few people can do—have courageous conversations with their clients that sometimes may even cost them business and relationships. People do not like to acknowledge their mortality, and it takes a courageous advisor to help them see that this conversation can determine whether or not a family is taken care of financially or not, should the primary income earner die unexpectedly.

This book is about these Miracle Merchants, their stories, and the product they place (how dare we say "sell")—life insurance. Every day, they do the right thing for the right reason. We say this with conviction because society, the media, and others often vilify this work, yet this group marches on. Why? Read on, and you will see why.

> **Society, the media, and others often vilify this work, yet this group marches on.**

It is because like the teacher, coach, mentor, parent, or leader…once in a great while, a student, player, mentee, or child…returns years later and tells the financial advisor, "I cannot imagine my life without you. You made a difference."

In this book are stories, history, and testimonials of people whose lives have been affected by special advisors who believe in the Miracle of Life Insurance, a product that—at the exact right moment—delivers relief, comfort, peace of mind, and dignity in a time of pain, suffering, grief, and confusion.

If you have the privilege of working with such an advisor, simply thank him or her; gratitude means the world to advisors. It inspires them and allows them to carry this good work forward to so many others.

And, to the advisors who were steeped in such training, be grateful for the mentors, firms, and companies that provided this for you. Unfortunately, the numbers of those who champion life insurance are dwindling, and the biggest losers are the people who won't have a relationship with such courageous and caring people. Without the intervention of these Miracle Merchants, most of us would never confront the need for life insurance and our mortality. Or if we did, it would be far too late in the game. We speak from the heart because we also would have fallen victim to denial and the alluring voices of the media sirens had it not been for those wise ones who came before us.

"Do you believe in miracles?" We do. We see them occur every day through the care, love, and compassion of life insurance-based financial advisors.

We also believe things happen for a reason. The reason you are reading this book at this very moment. The reason a financial advisor enters a client's life in an unusual and serendipitous way. The reason a person happens to "stumble" across this noble calling of ours. (Most eight-year-olds don't dream of becoming a financial advisor).

Let us simply be grateful it happened, carry on, and live a life worthy of the calling we have received. Let us keep our promises to those who matter.

CHAPTER 1
HOW WE GOT HERE

The insurance-based advisor is responsible for helping clients deal with two primary concerns:

1. *Living too long* and having their retirement savings run out before they die

2. *Dying too soon* and leaving their families without an income to live on in the absence of the primary income earner

These are the immediate threats that keep Americans up at night. The solution to the first issue is to establish and follow a sensible plan for saving and investing money. The solution to the second issue is to secure sufficient life insurance. This is the "difficult discussion" that so many advisors are avoiding.

MISCONCEPTIONS ABOUT THE COST OF INSURANCE

Americans are sadly uneducated about what life insurance is and what it costs.

LIMRA says **70 percent** of Americans failed a recent ten-question basic life insurance IQ test. And 83 percent of consumers say they don't purchase more life insurance because it's too expensive. But their perception of the cost is highly inflated; consumers believe life insurance costs nearly three times the actual price. In 2010, most Americans believed a twenty-year, $250,000-level term life policy for a healthy thirty-year-old would cost $400 a year. The actual cost was $150.[2]

Clients often resist buying life insurance because they do not have much money to spare. It is our job as financial advisors to help people understand that the small amount of money someone might spend on life insurance each month is not going to impact his or her standard of living massively. Is the amount you spend on coffee at your local coffee shop in a given month going to put you in a position where you are going to be unable to feed your children, lose your home, or have a massive hardship? Probably not. But if you were to die tomorrow, will that $3 million death benefit make a difference to the standard of living for your family? It definitely will.

> It is our job as financial advisors to help people understand that the $80 a month or so someone might spend on life insurance is not going to impact his or her standard of living massively.

It's the same with disability insurance. Is the monthly premium you pay right now going to make a material difference in your life? What would happen if you lost $15,000 a month in income? Would that have a material impact? When people say they can't buy insurance because they can't afford it or they have other things they want to spend their money on, many times it is because they haven't thought it through like this.

---

2. Corey Dahl, Brian Anderson, and Brian Gilbert, "The Shocking Statistics behind the Life Insurance Coverage Gap," LifeHealthPro website, http://www.lifehealthpro.com/2013/08/30/the-shocking-statistics-behind-the-life-insurance?t=life-sales-strategies&page=7.

The truth is, if your financial situation is such that $80 a month is going to dramatically impact your life, that tells us that you can't afford not to have life insurance.

PRIVATE CARS VS. THE JUNGLE

Why don't more advisors bring up the issue of risk management? Because, as we've mentioned, it' a difficult discussion. It becomes even more difficult when an advisor is happy and content.

We like to compare today's financial-advising career to having a private car. Our financial advisors are being driven around in beautiful, luxurious, well-stocked, private cars. They sit there enjoying good times, with seventy-two straight months of a bull market, without bringing up those difficult conversations with prospects and clients. But one hundred years ago, fifty years ago, selling insurance was the way agents made their living. They didn't spend time in private cars; they lived in a jungle where they ate only what they killed, so to speak.

If we truly want to help people, we will bring up the topic. But bringing it up once isn't enough. Even if clients say they agree with you and recognize the risk of being uninsured or underinsured, often they won't follow through with the application process. If you want to rest easily at night, you will do the difficult but right thing and give those clients a little bit of courage and backbone to get that insurance in place.

And securing the sufficient amount of insurance is just the beginning. It's critical to review your clients' coverage as their circumstances change.

When a young couple begins to have children, or when a couple opens a business or retires, their insurance needs change. It's our responsibility to ensure that their life coverage is sufficient at any given time in their lives.

HOW IT ALL STARTED

The first insurance company in the American colonies was formed in Charleston, South Carolina, in 1735. At first, the company offered only fire insurance. It added life insurance in 1760.

The panic of 1837 and the resulting financial crisis spurred a shift toward mutualization of life insurance companies. Between 1838 and 1849, only one life insurance company raised capital on a stock basis. During the same period, seventeen mutual companies, requiring little initial capital, were chartered. Many of today's largest life insurers were formed during this period, including New York Life, MassMutual, John Hancock, and MetLife.

In 1875, the Widows and Orphans Friendly Society was founded in Newark, New Jersey, with only one product: burial insurance. It was the first company in the United States to make life insurance available to the working class. That company eventually became Prudential.

Life insurance sales rose dramatically after World War I, peaking at $117 billion of insurance in force in 1930. By the eve of the Great Depression, more than 120 million life insurance policies were in force, equivalent to one policy for every man, woman, and child living in the United States at the time.

The end of World War II and the economic boom that followed boosted sales of life insurance in the United States. By the mid-1970s, 72 percent of the adult population of the United States and more than 90 percent of all husband-and-wife families owned some form of life insurance.[3] Sadly, as we mentioned earlier, more than 40 percent of American families have no life insurance in place today.

A SHIFT AWAY FROM RISK MANAGEMENT

Then, unfortunately, the focus began to shift away from life insurance toward other financial investment products.

When we hired people in the early 1970s, each advisor would have to spend the first fifteen to twenty minutes of every client interview explaining what financial planning was. Consumers had never heard of financial planning, so to them it was like hocus pocus. It was a brand-new industry nobody had ever heard of.

It wasn't the insurance companies that led us into financial planning; in fact, it was just the opposite. Insurance companies were dragged, kicking and screaming, by their ankles, into this financial-planning arena. They did not want to go there. They had a nice, comfortable life charging premiums that were two or three times what they need to charge today. They were happy, fat, and lazy.

In those days, all mutual-fund plans were contractual plans. So I would sell you a plan for $100 a month for ten years, and I would show you what your plan would look like at the end of ten years, after you put in $12,000. In the first year, each time you made a $100 deposit, I got a $50 commission. So the first year, you would put in $1,200, and I got $600. Those contractual plans were ultimately declared illegal. Then regulations were passed, limiting a dealer's first-year total compensation to 8.3 percent. If you put in $1,200, we got about $100 out of that $1,200 sale. Today, that number is 1 percent or less, and declining.

Insurance companies are not abandoning the product; the problem is that distribution is not being compensated to deliver it anymore. The distributors—not the life insurance companies—are leaving the battlefield. That means advisors are getting paid less to sell life insurance now.

3. Corey Dahl, "A Brief History of Life Insurance," September 9, 2013, LifeHealthPro website, http://www.lifehealthpro.com/2013/09/09/a-brief-history-of-life-insurance?t=life-products&page=3.

Competitive forces, market demands, and regulatory changes have created the need to deliver products in more effective ways while managing costs. Prolonged low interest rates have put pressure on carriers. One way they can manage their balance sheets is to raise product rates; another way is to cut back on distribution. We've seen carriers reduce distribution within both the career channel and the broker channel in an effort to limit sales of these capital-intensive products.[4]

With the shift toward financial planning, asset accumulation, and equity areas, there just isn't enough emphasis on life insurance today.

It is a tragedy that many advisors who once believed in life insurance have all but abandoned it—and some have never recognized its importance as the anchor of every financial plan. For many advisors who once sold life insurance, as their practices matured, they felt a pull toward the securities world, and their revenues started becoming stronger from that side of the business. Then the life insurance side of their business died. For an advisor, a focus on life insurance is like a muscle—if it is not worked, it deteriorates. Unfortunately, a lot of advisors in our industry have let the "life insurance muscle" atrophy because they have not flexed it enough.

We would like to see those advisors get back on track with selling the Miracle of Life Insurance. We have a responsibility and obligation to our clients to have that conversation with them.

We cannot help but wonder if advisors who gravitate away from life insurance were ever fully aware of the power it has to secure a family's financial future. Maybe they just sold it in the beginning of their careers because they had to do so to validate contracts. A lot of the advisors whose practices have migrated to securities are the ones who never really bought into life insurance. We have had constant battles trying to get them to realize its value. Too many of them look at how it might benefit them, not their clients.

THE TIPPING POINT: SHAUN'S MOTHER'S STORY

Financial advisors who have had a personal experience with the Miracle of Life Insurance—whether with family members, friends, or clients—tend to be the strongest advocates for life insurance. Once you witness the power of life insurance personally, it is a "tipping point." When an income earner whom you work with dies and has life insurance in place, you will never forget the feeling of relief the surviving family members have upon realizing that they will be okay in the future, at least financially.

Likewise, when an income earner whom you work with dies and does not have life insurance in place—or becomes disabled and does not have long-term-care insurance in place—you will never forget the feeling of despair the survivors feel upon realizing that they face not only emotional hardship but also financial hardship.

---

4. Dan Mulé, "The Brave New World of Life Insurance Distribution," February 4, 2014, LifeHealthPro website, http://www.lifehealthpro.com/2014/02/04/the-brave-new-world-of-life-insurance-distribution?t=practice-management&page=2.

As financial advisors who understand the urgency and dire need for insurance, it might seem that those people in our lives would be the most fully insured people around. Unfortunately, that is not the case.

Sometimes the people we love and the people who are the closest to us are the ones we have the most difficult time persuading and influencing about the urgent need for insurance.

This story about the mother of Shaun McDuffee, one of this book's authors, demonstrates several facets of the reality of this topic that we discuss in this book:

1. People's denial that they will ever get sick or die prematurely
2. The incredible difficulty of bringing the subject up in a conversation
3. The devastating result when people do not secure the insurance they need, long before they think they might need it

Here is Shaun's story.

My grandmother on my mother's side died of Alzheimer's disease. Her in-home nursing care cost $60,000 a year, and then she went into a skilled-nursing facility that cost hundreds of thousands of dollars. After my grandmother passed, I told my mother, "Mom, I'm going to get you a long-term-care policy, and I will pay for it. I don't want you to feel ever in the future that you are a financial burden or that your legacy money is getting eaten up because of a medical condition."

She replied, "Absolutely not. I don't want long-term-care coverage. I am not filling out the applications. I have a plan in place; I belong to the Hemlock Society. If something like that happens to me, it will be taken care of. There won't be a long-term-care event."

The Hemlock Society is an organization that was founded in 1980 to support legislation permitting physician-assisted dying. In 2003, the organization renamed itself. In 2004, it merged with another group and became a national organization called Compassion & Choices.

She basically was telling me that if she became sick, she would just commit suicide or have somebody euthanize her. I said, "You have got to be kidding me. That is your plan? Number one, I am outraged that you would share something that stupid with me, and number two, the reality is that that isn't a plan." Like Mike Tyson said, "We all have a plan until we get punched in the mouth."

"WE ALL HAVE A PLAN UNTIL WE GET PUNCHED IN THE MOUTH."

I went back and forth with her on this for three months. She didn't have to pay for the policy. She didn't have to do anything, but she refused to sign the paperwork or acknowledge that something could happen to her. Well, sadly, my mother got Alzheimer's disease, just like her mother did, and her plan didn't pan out. For the past four years, I have been spending $100,000 a year on her care. The premium for that long-term-care policy she refused to let me buy would have cost $343 a month, which is only $4,116 a year.

I don't know how many people in America can afford $100,000 a year in care on top of their normal living expenses and withstand the impact that would have on their retirement. I am blessed that this industry provided me with the income to help her. Otherwise, she would be living with me, and I would probably be divorced because my wife would have gone bonkers trying to help take care of my mother. It is just an awful situation.

I am fairly good at intervening and helping people have difficult discussions and make tough decisions, but I couldn't get through to one of the people who is closest to me.

My failure to get her to do what she needed to do is really only impacting me. But it has been an impetus to make sure that when I am talking to clients, a similar situation doesn't happen for them or someone they love.

I finally gave up after months of arguing with her. That is the moral of the story for financial advisors: don't ever give up. You are going to deal with some people who are unreasonable. And sadly, my mother is one of them.

COMING SOON: THE FIDUCIARY STANDARD

Not only is it our moral responsibility to help our clients manage risk; it could become the law. In this country and in many other countries around the world, new fiduciary standards are being enacted. These new regulations are being enforced to protect consumers from unscrupulous financial advisors who recommend financial decisions based on their own profit potential.

The bottom line is that someday we will all be required by law to advise clients in a way that's in their best interest. If you are my client, and I do not point out the risk involved with your being uninsured or underinsured, one could argue that I'm not doing what is in your best interest.

CHAPTER 2

HUMAN LIFE VALUE— WHAT IS YOUR LIFE WORTH?

When we insure a person's life, the goal is to provide enough coverage to replace the amount of money he or she could earn throughout an entire lifetime. That is the loss the family will suffer if that primary income earner dies prematurely, and we refer to it as "human life value."

THE CONCEPT OF HUMAN LIFE VALUE IS BORN

Solomon Huebner, PhD, is considered "the father of insurance education." A professor at The Wharton School of the University of Pennsylvania, he taught the first course ever given in insurance, established Wharton's insurance department, and became the architect of the modern financial services industry.

In 1959, Huebner wrote *The Economics of Life Insurance*. In that book, he takes a deep dive into the perspective of the household as a business entity. A family is a revenue-producing business entity and has to deal with budgets and risk management. The tool that can be leveraged and used better than any other resource out there is life insurance. Huebner was the first one to say that human life value is the formula that should be used to determine the proper amount of life insurance for that risk-management component.

PEOPLE DRASTICALLY UNDERESTIMATE THEIR INSURANCE NEEDS

Most people in our industry are no longer talking about human life value—a person's replacement value. And many of the advisors who *are* still talking about life insurance are becoming more like order-takers than they are advisors or guides. They will write a policy for the amount the client asks for but fail to explain how much life insurance is really sufficient, based on the family's situation.

Most people think that if their employer offers them life insurance, and they get life insurance worth two times their annual salary, they are covered sufficiently. Often, that is not nearly enough life insurance to cover a person's human life value.

Recently I (Shaun) got a call from a young physician. He and his wife had attended a dinner I hosted for prospective clients four years ago. He was just starting his medical practice. He bought some life insurance while completing his residency program and remembered my talk about human life value. He and his wife had $1 million in life insurance but knew they needed more coverage because they now have two young children, with a third one on the way. The husband makes $400,000 a year now.

I told them that right now, that million-dollar policy will replace about $30,000 to $50,000 of income a year, if they're lucky. To replace $400,000 in income, at a bare minimum they need $8 million to $10 million in life insurance. And then I walked them through it. I told them that if he were sued in a wrongful-death situation,

> To replace $400,000 in income, at a bare minimum they need $8 million to $10 million in life insurance.

the attorneys are simply going to take the numbers from a human life value table. They would start with the low end of the human life value calculation to decide on the settlement. This doctor is thirty-three years old. At that age, the table is going to start out at about thirty times his current income. That means that in a wrongful-death case, his attorneys will start negotiations at $12 million. Insurance companies will not insure a person for his or her full human life value. We could fairly easily get him twenty times his annual income with most carriers, which means we could probably get him $8 million to $10 million as a settlement. That is the amount he needs to replace his human life value.

> **The goal is to get life insurance coverage that's as close to your human life value as you can because that is the economic loss to your family if you were to die.**

The goal is to get life insurance coverage that's as close to your human life value as you can because that is the economic loss to your family if you were to die. Not many advisors are having that difficult discussion—to tell a thirty-three-year-old physician that he or she needs $8 million to $10 million in life insurance.

At first, people are shocked to find out how much coverage they need to replace their life value. But once you walk them through it, they understand how life insurance works and why they need that amount.

To assess the financial loss your family would incur if you were to die unexpectedly, try out the interactive human life value calculator on the Life Happens website at http://www.lifehappens.org/insurance-calculators/calculate-human-life-value/.

CHAPTER 3
LIFE INSURANCE AS AN INVESTMENT

Not only does life insurance pay a death benefit to your beneficiaries upon your death; you also can use the cash value from certain types of insurance as an investment to help increase your quality of life while you're still alive.

Financial advisors often refer to the "cash-value component" as a benefit of a permanent life insurance policy. This means that if you own a permanent life insurance policy, you will not pay taxes on any interest, dividends, or capital gains in the policy until you withdraw the proceeds. (You get similar tax deferral benefits with retirement accounts such as IRAs and 401(k) plans.)

Using the cash value from permanent life insurance as an investment doesn't make sense for everyone, but it can pay off for some people.

PERMANENT VS. TERM LIFE INSURANCE

In all the death claims we've delivered, no one has ever asked us what type of insurance was in place. The only question people ask is, "Is this the most we can get?"

The focus of this book is *why* life insurance is critical, not the various types of insurance. So we don't want to get too technical about this topic. But we do want to mention the importance of ensuring that at least some of your life insurance is *permanent* (vs. term) and that your coverage is convertible.

Here is the difference between term and permanent (perm) life insurance.

With *term life insurance*, you are paying the insurance company to transfer the risk that you will die during the stated term of the policy. If you have a twenty-year term policy, your premiums are guaranteed to stay the same for twenty years. If you die during that twenty-year period, the insurance company will pay the death benefit to your beneficiaries. But if you get to the end of your twenty-year policy and are still alive, no one will receive a cash payout. (You didn't waste the money on those premiums, however; you had peace of mind during that twenty-year period. You knew that if something had happened to you, your beneficiaries would have received a death benefit.)

In contrast, *permanent life insurance* is designed to exist you until your death. Because the insurance company is likely to pay a death benefit in this case, the premiums cost more than those for term insurance. But permanent insurance policies often include a tax-advantaged component, so a part of your premium is set aside to accrue for your potential future use.

Permanent life insurance pays 100 percent as long as the policy remains in force. Term insurance pays about 2 percent of the time—98 percent of time, the policy isn't in force because the policyholder lives past the end of the term.

We emphatically believe that every person needs to be insured to his or her human life value. If your limited cash flow makes term insurance your only possible option right now, that's fine—just make sure you consider a convertible product so that you protect your insurability and have the ability to convert it to permanent life insurance later, which you may have the ability to do without the need for underwriting. If you have $5 million worth of convertible term insurance and have a major heart attack, you have the option to convert a portion or the full face amount to perm insurance at the same rates as your original policy.

We strongly recommend that you meet with your financial advisor to determine the right amount and types of coverage for you and your family.

THE PERMISSION SLIP

Physicians in their sixties and seventies who had the foresight to buy permanent insurance early on have options that other people their age don't.

When I (Phil) first came into this business in 1962, Maury Stewart, who hired me, used to say, "Don't take your bread money to the poker game." In other words, set aside the money you need for the essentials in life, and don't fritter it away on nonessentials.

When you have taken care of the risk-management part of the equation and have cash value in a life insurance policy, you may feel comfortable going farther out on the risk line than you otherwise could. With your risk covered, now you may be more venturesome in your investments in real estate, individual stocks in your portfolio, or junk bonds that pay a higher interest rate, for example. Get the safety net—life insurance—in place first.

"DON'T TAKE YOUR BREAD MONEY TO THE POKER GAME."

Your goals will change over the next twenty years, so a twenty-year term insurance policy may not meet your long-term needs. Give yourself the option to convert some or all of your insurance into permanent life insurance; don't box yourself in. Buying the cheapest term product covers your insurance needs now, but you are putting yourself in a box down the road by taking that approach.

Permanent insurance is a critical part of any financial plan, legacy plan, or estate plan. We hear people say, "I've got twenty-year term insurance. I'm good." They might be good for twenty years, but they're not great for the long haul. If that is all they have in place, they have just eliminated a lot of options for themselves later in life. And we have a saying about this: "When we get to retirement, he or she with the most options wins."

When you own permanent life insurance, it provides you with the potential to maximize your retirement income, provide a comfortable future for your children and grandchildren, and leave a legacy.

LIFE INSURANCE TAX BENEFIT: A FAVORITE TAX-REFORM TOPIC

In 1990, the Government Accounting Office (GAO) released a report about tax-deferred growth in life insurance products. The report said, "The interest that is earned on life insurance policies and deferred annuity contracts, commonly referred to as 'inside buildup,' is not taxed as long as it accumulates within the contract. By choosing not to tax the interest as it is earned, the federal government forgoes an estimated $5 billion in tax revenue each year."

So in the Technical and Miscellaneous Revenue Act of 1988, Congress asked the GAO to examine the policy justification for, and implications of, this tax treatment. Congress also asked the GAO to study how effectively the revised (narrowed) definition of life insurance in the new law restricted the sale of investment-oriented life insurance products.

In chapter 4 of the report, the GAO made this recommendation to Congress:

> Because the pattern of policy usage as well as the type of products offered can change, Congress may want to periodically reconsider its policy decision to grant preferential tax treatment to inside buildup, weighing the social benefits against the revenue forgone.

> If Congress decides not to tax inside buildup, then GAO recommends that Congress eliminate tax-free borrowing of life insurance proceeds. Any borrowing of these proceeds should be considered a distribution of interest income. To offset the advantages of accruing interest income without tax, a penalty provision needs to be added to the regular tax. Since repayment of the amount borrowed restores the death benefits, any amount that is taxed when it is borrowed should be tax-deductible if subsequently repaid.[5]

5. "Tax Treatment of Life Insurance and Annuity Accrued Interest," January 1990, Government Accounting Office website, http://www.gao.gov/assets/150/148632.pdf.

The tax-deferred benefit is still allowed, although reducing or eliminating the benefit is a favorite topic among many legislators. Critics claim that the "inside buildup" incentive benefits the wealthy, and they want that interest to become subject to income tax.

But our industry knows that giving people an extra incentive to buy life insurance motivates them to buy insurance that protects their spouses and children.

TRANSFER YOUR WEALTH TO YOUR FAMILY, NOT TO THE GOVERNMENT

Many people work diligently to save money all their lives. But if they don't plan properly as they build up their assets, the government will remove a chunk of those assets when the primary income earner dies.

One of our clients is a physician who is about to turn seventy years old. When he turns 70½, he will have to comply with federal required minimum distributions in his individual retirement accounts (IRAs) and 401(k) retirement plan. He and his wife have $12 million in assets. They wanted to pass that money along to their grandchildren. But with the financial plan they had, they would have been able to pass along only about $2.5 to $3 million of that money to their grandkids. In this case, the client had the ability to pass along a substantial amount of money to his heirs by way of a second life insurance policy.

With life insurance, you can use pennies or dimes to pay many dollars' worth of taxes. That leverage you get with life insurance, especially if you purchase it early on, is tremendous. By leveraging life insurance, a competent financial planner can help clients reduce taxes owed at death.

One of our long-time clients who understands this concept extremely well helped his business partner understand it recently.

One of our clients—let's call him Rick—was visiting with one of his partners over lunch one day. We'll call him Dan. Dan said he was just getting killed in taxes. He had just received a 1099 from his investment portfolio and found out that he had to come up with a significant amount of money to cover the taxes attributed to his portfolio gains for the year. Rick, our client, explained that this is one of the reasons he chose to overfund his life insurance product as a supplement for retirement. Dan asked, "Why would you ever use life insurance as an investment? The costs are outrageous, and everything goes to fees and commissions."

Rick thought about it for a minute and replied that everything has costs. He told Dan, "In fact, by your own admission, your portfolio generated significant costs last year. I am pretty sure that my insurance costs this year were far below what you paid."

Then Rick asked Dan, "What are you getting from the government for those significant costs?"

Dan replied, "Basically nothing."

Rick said, "Well, I am certain that I paid much less than that in costs this year, and my family is going to get a large sum of money when I die. I'm pretty sure I have a better deal."

Two weeks later, Dan called our client, Rick, to discuss this concept in detail, primarily because of the simple way Rick explained the "cost/benefit" concept to him.

Not enough financial advisors understand this concept, and that is a tragedy because it is the most critical component of a financial plan. When we explain it to them, it resonates with them, but they don't often change their approach to focus on life insurance. They will say, "I used to talk to clients about that, but I've been so focused on helping them with accumulation of assets, I haven't talked about leveraging life insurance."

The purpose of this book is to remind advisors and consumers alike that life insurance should be the anchor of any financial plan and motivate financial advisors to commit to helping clients get life insurance in place.

We want to challenge each financial advisor to ask himself or herself, "Am I really doing comprehensive financial planning?" We think that failing to address life insurance with clients is verging on malpractice. It is our moral obligation to help our clients understand risk management and the way life insurance covers it.

CHAPTER 4

AN ORGANIZATION DEVOTED TO THE IMPORTANCE OF LIFE INSURANCE

LIFE HAPPENS.

A NONPROFIT ORGANIZATION

Back in 1994, seven leading insurance producer companies recognized the need to better educate the public about important insurance planning topics. They formed an organization called the LIFE Foundation. A few years ago, the organization changed its name to Life Happens. Today, more than 140 of the nation's leading insurance and financial services organizations provide financial support to help Life Happens publicize its educational messages about the critical role life insurance plays in people's lives.

Life Happens is a valuable third-party resource that can help advisors be more effective in delivering products to an extremely underinsured public.

On its website (www.lifehappens.org), the organization offers calculators that can help you determine how much life insurance you need, how much disability insurance you need, and how to calculate your human life value.

The average adult American, according to LIMRA International, has about $170,000 of insurance coverage, approximately four times their annual income. Obviously they will be dead for more than four years. The Life Happens calculator helps determine what it will take to save a business or protect one's family.

Life Happens also educates people about the importance of securing disability insurance. Their research has discovered these facts:

- One-third of individuals over the age of thirty will suffer a disability lasting three months or longer.

- Nearly half of home foreclosures are caused by an unforeseen disability.

- Most disabilities are the result of illnesses, not accidents.

- Two-thirds of those who apply for Social Security disability are denied benefits.

There are four reasons to use Life Happens as a resource:

1. Their easy-to-understand content helps the public understand insurance topics in nontechnical terminology.

2. Consumers trust their information because it is coming from a nonprofit third party, not a specific insurance company or advisor. So it has a lot of credibility.

3. The organization does not promote either term or permanent insurance but instead focuses on ensuring that people secure enough life insurance to cover their human life value. They provide a calculator for this purpose on their website.

4. Life Happens conveys stories (Real Life Stories) about people whose lives have changed for the better because a family's primary income earner planned ahead and took out life insurance. The purchase of life insurance is both a rational and emotional decision; these stories help you describe the impact life insurance can have on people's lives.

Simply log on to www.lifehappens.org to review these resources, and refer your prospects and clients to the site too.

CHAPTER 5

HOW OUR INSURANCE NEEDS CHANGE OVER TIME

The Kinder Brothers, who have provided sales-management-consulting and training tools to our industry for decades, often say that life insurance not only makes sense at every stage of life but serves as the financial cornerstone of one's financial plan and is an asset class all by itself.

People need life insurance for every stage of life, and as their personal situations change, their life insurance needs change too.

Most people will need more life insurance when they reach sixty-five than they need at age thirty-five. Times have changed, and people are living much longer than we used to, but many advisors are still selling life insurance as if people are going to die at sixty-five years of age. With today's mortality tables, people need long-term, permanent life insurance.

Current statistics show that for every one hundred people starting their careers at age twenty-five, by the time they are sixty-five, only thirteen will be dead. That means eighty-seven are still alive. There's a good chance that they'll need more life insurance then than they do now. They will need personal life insurance. The old axiom is still true that people are going to die before sixty-five or after sixty-five—one or the other. Most will die after sixty-five. The older they get, the more needs they have. We want to sell life insurance for all stages of life.

We want to sell life insurance for all stages of life.

The outline on the next page shows how life insurance needs change at every stage in life. It is interesting that the older we get, the more options and choices we have regarding life insurance. The common belief that a person doesn't need it beyond his or her child-rearing years is simply not true. This chart demonstrates that life insurance plays an even bigger role at life's later stages. If you are a financial advisor, do the right thing by talking to your clients about the world of options life insurance opens up at these later life stages. Also do the right thing by talking to your younger clients about life insurance so they can lock in affordable permanent premiums that will provide a host of options later on.

LIFE INSURANCE GENERAL CONSIDERATIONS

Children	Single People	Married People with No Children	Married People with Children	Empty Nesters	Seniors
Guaranteed insurability	Guaranteed insurability				
Cash value accumulation	Cash value accumulation	Cash value accumulation	Cash value accumulation	Cash value accumulation	
Final expenses	Final expenses	Final expenses	Final expenses	Final expenses	Final expenses
Lower premiums	Lower premiums				
	Debt protection	Debt protection	Debt protection	Debt protection	Debt protection
		Mortgage acceleration	Mortgage acceleration	Mortgage acceleration	Mortgage acceleration
		Income needs	Income needs	Income needs	Income needs
		Lifestyle protection	Lifestyle protection	Lifestyle protection	Lifestyle protection
			Funding for future emergencies	Funding for future emergencies	Funding for future emergencies
			Education fund		
				Pension maximization	Pension maximization
				Social Security offset	Social Security offset
				Replacement of group insurance	Replacement of group insurance
				Gifts	Gifts
					Equalization of inheritances
					Legacy/charity
					Wealth replacement
					Dynasty trust funding

CHAPTER 6

FINANCIAL ADVISORS ARE MIRACLE MERCHANTS

At North Star Resource Group, we are committed to ensuring that our clients know about the Miracle of Life Insurance—how it can protect family members' financial future in the event of the primary income earner's death. As we mentioned in the introduction, we consider our financial advisors who sell life insurance to be "Miracle Merchants." They are merchants who are selling a miracle.

The definition of a sale is "the transfer of one's beliefs and enthusiasm to another." Do you believe you make an incredible difference in your clients' lives? You do. Think about where they would be without you.

All too often, though, there are obstacles to getting that miracle in force for our clients. Again most clients do not like to discuss their mortality, so most advisors do not like to bring up the difficult subject. There are other obstacles too.

The book *Rediscovering Catholicism: Journeying Toward Our Spiritual North Star* by Matthew Kelly reminds us that, regardless of one's religious views or spiritual beliefs, many times, religious readings provide powerful teachings and lessons that are beneficial. Kelly's book is no exception to that rule—the very first chapter provides some takeaways that we refer to often.

He proposes that the world has three very constant and present enemies that prevent us from having fulfilling and meaningful lives:

1. **Individualism**—Always being concerned with only how *we* benefit from anything we engage in. It is the ultimate "What's in it for me?" mind-set.

2. **Hedonism**—Always focusing on and building priorities around satisfying short-term needs and pleasures. It is the ultimate example of the "If it feels good, do it!" mind-set.

3. **Minimalism**—Always looking for the easiest path. It is the ultimate "What is the least amount I can do to get the most?" mind-set.

All of us can acknowledge that we have fallen victim at some point to these dangers in both our personal and professional lives. We believe these are also the "enemies" that our clients face when dealing with their own financial plans and financial futures.

Over the past few years, in working with and managing client relationships, behaviors, and expectations, we have shared this message numerous times. It helps explain the behavioral component of our profession.

Let's take a closer look at these three dangerous mind-sets.

INDIVIDUALISM

Individualism is often present at the very onset of the client/advisor relationship. It is when clients are trying to ascertain what's in it for them if they work with the advisor. Sometimes, a client considers being a "do-it-yourselfer" to save some money. This short-term-focused perspective can best be summarized as being "penny-wise and pound-

> **Clients typically do not have the foresight to insure themselves with the adequate amount or the urgency to put the plan in action today.**

foolish." Paying somewhere in the neighborhood of 1 percent annually to have the assurance of a professional advisor guiding you in starting and staying the course of financial security is well worth it. Without the guidance of an advisor, most clients will not have the sense of urgency to start now—they will postpone the decision to apply for life insurance. Clients typically do not have the foresight to insure themselves with the adequate amount or the urgency to put the plan in action today. Their intentions are excellent, but they are fighting human nature and emotions.

We need to be mindful of the investment vs. investor return number that Dalbar publishes. In the most recent JP Morgan advisor guide to the markets, the twenty-year holding period of 1996 to 2015 showed investor return in the S&P 500 at 8.2 percent. Investor return based on inflows and outflows in the index was 2.1 percent. As usual, the "behavior" factor accounted for the historic 6 to 7 percent difference—the difference that financial advisors make. (Past performance is not indicative of future results. One cannot invest an index.)

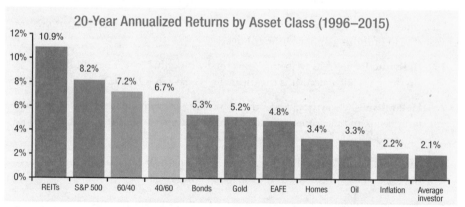

Source: J.P. Morgan Asset Management, Dalbar Inc.Indexes used are as follows: REITS: AREIT Equity REIT Index. EAFE: MSCI EAFE, Oil: WTI Index, Bonds: Barclays U.S. Aggregate Index. Homes: median sale price of existing single-family homes. Gold: USD/troy oz. Inflation: CPI. 60/40: A balanced portfolio with 60% invested in S&P 500 Index and 40% invested in high-quality US fixed income, represented by the Barclays US Aggregate Index. The portfolio is rebalanced annually. Average asset allocation investor return is based on an analysis by Dalbar Inc., which utilizes the net of aggregate mutual fund sales, redemptions, and exchanges each month as a measure of investor behavior. Returns are annualized (and total return where applicable) and represent the 20-year period ending 12/31/15 to match Dalbar's most recent analysis. Guide to the Markets—US Data—are as of June 30, 2016.

HEDONISM

Hedonism is the belief that pleasure or happiness is the most important goal in life. It attacks our clients in the realm of instant gratification. Perhaps nothing steals a financially secure and independent future greater than hedonism. The barrage of the thousands of ways our clients can part from their hard-earned money every day is only countered by the voice an advisor brings to the conversation. It is the voice that tries to balance the scales of enjoying today yet saving and making some sacrifices for tomorrow. It is the notion of "Are you spending your tomorrows or buying them?"

The world we live in is one of instant gratification—if it looks good, feels good, or tastes good, do it, and do it now! That is the thunder the media and advertisers push out to us all day, every day. How does one stand a chance without regular conversations, educational messaging, and most importantly, the discipline and focus on the end result—the plan that an advisor brings to the relationship? If an advisor is not involved, hedonism will clearly win the day. Worse yet, clients will lose in their pursuit to never outlive their money and to be prepared when the uncertainties of life occur.

MINIMALISM

Minimalism is most often seen in the expectations many people have of their financial advisors. Because of the delay many have in addressing their financial future, they are often in a position of playing "catch-up." Middle-aged people tend to get a later start on things, and by that time, most of them are accustomed to a certain lifestyle. This leads to clients putting a much higher degree of pressure and expectations on the advisor to "make up" for the lost time and for a lack of discipline, focus, and hedonistic priorities that clients have had. In essence, the client is saying to the advisor, "What is the very least I can put in the get the most out?"

We believe that there is a time and place to have a minimalistic mind-set, but it needs to be in areas of little importance or consequence. Where we should never have this type of mind-set is with our relationships, spirituality, health, education, career, and financial matters. Just imagine walking through life trying to put the least in and getting the most out of these areas. Imagine the outcome advisors would have in this career if we took the approach of "What is the least I can put in?" None of us would be here. We took the opposite approach—we went *all in*. And that is the same mind-set clients need to cross the finish line. They can't hold back and expect advisors to be the miracle workers who make up for their transgressions. They need to fully cooperate and listen to their advisors' advice and wisdom and also develop the discipline and make the sacrifices necessary to hit their goals. That happens only when an advisor is involved. It is a real shame to take a minimalist approach with one's financial future. A person couldn't start off on a worse foundation.

These three dangers are very real threats to our clients reaching their financial and life goals and plans. Many will expect us to be miracle workers, but try as we may, we simply are not. We are, however, miracle merchants. Every day, we sell our wisdom, products, and services, and those who heed our advice and are *all in* will enjoy the miracle of multigenerational financial independence and security.

Financial advisors are like thermostats. Here's how. A *thermometer* simply measures and reports the temperature. That's what many clients do on their own. But a *thermostat* controls, manages, sets, and regulates the temperature. It takes positive action to create an ideal environment.

Be the thermostat that creates an environment for your clients that is ideal for protecting the future.

CHAPTER 7

ADVISORS ARE INTERVENTION SPECIALISTS

You have probably seen the TV shows about families who conduct "interventions" to try to get loved ones to seek help for a drug or alcohol addiction before it kills them. As advisors, we must do interventions with clients. Every advisor should view himself or herself as an "intervention specialist." Nothing happens until we start the conversation, send the e-mail, and ask for the meeting.

WHY THE DISCUSSION IS URGENT

We need to gently plant the seed in people's minds that, regardless of the best intentions they have for themselves and their family members' future, they must take action *today*. Every day they delay does the following:

1. Further exposes them to risk because they are not addressing risk management with life insurance

2. Costs them the miracle of potential compounding interest

3. Makes it more difficult to secure sufficient coverage because they get older and run the risk of being diagnosed with health problems that could cause them to be declined for insurance

4. Leaves them without the peace of mind, assurance, and comfort associated with knowing they are truly living up to their responsibilities and obligations

Even when clients *start* their journey on the path to financial security, it is not certain that they will *stay* on the right path. Distractions stand in their way of staying on course. For example, they often fall victim to the sweet sounds of market timing and to the media sirens that give them doubts about which products to select.

> Even when clients *start* their journey on the path to financial security, it is not certain that they will *stay* on the right path.

What every client and prospective client needs is an advisor much like Ulysses in *The Iliad*, who knew his sailors would become their own worst enemies and would succumb to the siren's song. So he tied each one down to the mast of the ship to keep them out of harm's way.

How large would your client base be if you waited for people to approach you? We all know the answer. In that situation, most advisors' practices would be substantially smaller than the robust and productive practices that so many advisors have or are in the midst of building.

It is comforting and reassuring when an advisor fully understands the psychology behind this first role and responsibility. We have yet to meet anyone who does not have good intentions for their money by spending less and saving more. Just about everyone plans on doing something about helping their children with higher-education funding. And who doesn't believe in having the resources to have choices later on in life to retire or rewire, to be in a financial position to make work an option instead of having to work?

WHEN PEOPLE BEGIN TO WORRY ABOUT IT

Intentions are pretty much worthless! It takes action and implementation to get results. The challenge is the way the Good Lord hardwired us. We have been predisposed to be natural procrastinators. We think we have *plenty of time* to do all of those noble things listed above. When does someone begin to have a sense of urgency around these matters? Usually when it is too late. The sense of urgency for people comes when:

1. They look in the mirror and realize they are not getting any younger and are closer to age seventy than they are to forty.

2. They see their children getting drivers' licenses and begin to realize they are growing up and college is drawing nearer.

3. They are diagnosed with an illness that causes them to get serious about financially protecting those they love.

4. They attend funerals, weddings, and retirement parties and realize that one day those events will happen to them.

So, for a brief but fleeting moment, they think about doing something. But even then, not much happens because those moments come and go. The intention does not become a reality or action, and they slip back into the normal routines of life. Everyone has good intentions, but realistically, the only way action is ever taken is if there is intervention. It requires *your* intervention. You, the advisor, bring the sense of urgency. It requires you to have a conversation with people. *You* need to send an e-mail inviting them to an upcoming educational dinner. It is the phone call *you* make to ask them to have a cup of coffee and take a few minutes to discuss making sure they don't outlive their money. *You* have to ask them to pause and think about just what this world will look like the day they are no longer a part of it. That day is guaranteed to occur. People with families should have the sense of responsibility to think about what will happen to those they love who will be left in this world without them.

If you don't intervene, it won't happen. And if by chance it does happen to some degree, it won't be as effective and impactful if you are not involved in their planning process. Even if they managed to do some basic planning and prepare on their own, they would still have gone a lot further and a lot faster with your help, guidance, and wisdom.

> One of the most important journeys clients must take in their lifetime is to address their financial stability and security.

Arguably, one of the most important journeys clients must take in their lifetime is to address their financial stability and security. Hoping for the very best future won't make it happen; they have to prepare for best- and worst-case scenarios. When you, as an advisor, realize that journey will never occur if you don't intervene, it overwhelms you with the confidence and conviction to take action. It gives you the courage to bring up the subject no one wants to talk about. Our career provides you with the three I's: impact, independence, and income. You enjoy all of those things because you have the courage to ask and intervene.

If you were to ask every one of your clients if they could go back in time and change anything about their financial plan, what would it be? We are confident that one of the top answers would be, "I wish I had started planning sooner." So what prevented them from starting sooner? You! They had not met you yet. And when they did meet you, their lives and their families' lives changed for the better, forever. You have the ability every day to be part of the solution for your clients and society.

In this country, more than two-thirds of our $17 trillion deficit is dedicated to entitlement programs. Americans would not rely so heavily on these programs if they had someone like you in their lives earlier. People need your wisdom. They want your guidance. They just have this little thing called human nature that prevents them from walking up to you and saying, "Save me, help me, guide me." It just won't happen.

But please do not let that stand in your way. See it as your role, your responsibility, to be the intervention specialist. Always remember that intervention must occur for implementation.

Take comfort and pride that every day you carry with you a secret and a solution.

AN INTERVENTION IN WRITING

Having sufficient life insurance at every stage of life is one of the most responsible and intelligent decisions a person can make.

But LIMRA found that one in three affluent households earning more than $100,000 per year have insufficient insurance coverage. Half of all US households (58 million households) say they need more coverage; this is the highest level LIMRA has ever reported.

Several years ago, one of our advisors, Doug Weisenberger, received a letter at home from State Farm asking him to review his auto insurance to ensure that he had enough homeowner's insurance. He took that idea and created his own letter to send to clients, asking them to evaluate whether or not they had enough life insurance coverage.

Here is the letter Doug started sending out to his clients, after having it compliance-approved:

Client Life Benefits Letter

[Printed on company letterhead]

Date

Name of client

Address

Dear _____:

As a service to our clients, we are contacting you to ensure that you have adequate life insurance coverage. Our records show that you have $x,xxx,xxx of life protection in force. This will provide $x,xxx per month to your family in the event of your untimely death.

If you have more coverage than our records show, please let us know so we can update our records. If this amount is correct, but you feel it may be insufficient to cover your risks, please call us, and we will set up a time to review your needs and develop a solution.

I can be reached at [phone and e-mail address].

Best regards,

Advisor Name

When will you send a letter or e-mail like this to all of your clients? We suggest that you meet with your administration team and set up a time frame to launch a letter like this. A great time to remind people to check their coverage is in September, which is Life Insurance Awareness Month. This is a valuable service you can provide for your clients.

September

SUNDAY	MONDAY	TUESDAY	WEDNESDAY	THURSDAY	FRIDAY	SATURDAY
				1	2	3
4	5	6	7	8	9	10
11	12	13	14	15	16	17
18	19	20	21	22	23	24
25	26	27	28	29	30	

ERADICATE VOCATIONAL IRONY

Many professionals fall into the trap of "vocational irony." That is when a person who is trained in a certain vocation fails to take his or own professional advice. An example is the doctor who smokes two packs of cigarettes a day. Another is the nutrition expert who is overweight.

Vocational irony occurs when a professional is very good at his or her profession but is completely unable or unwilling to use this ability to help his or her own family.

In essence, it is the age-old story about "the cobbler whose children had no shoes." The cobbler was so busy making shoes for the entire village that he neglected the needs of his very own children. Unfortunately, many advisors, despite knowing the critical importance of securing life insurance, have insufficient coverage.

Let's be great role models to the clients we serve and live according to our own advice.

CHAPTER 8

ADVISORS ARE THE ANGELS AMONG US

At Christmas time, we enjoy watching the holiday classic, *It's a Wonderful Life*, filmed in 1941 and starring the legendary Jimmy Stewart as George Bailey.

George Bailey, after a life of sacrifices for others, gets pushed over the edge when his absentminded uncle's mistake puts the family business in dire straits. George is about to take his life, knowing that all can be resolved with the proceeds of his $15,000 life insurance policy. George Bailey believes he is worth more dead than alive. Right before he takes the plunge off a bridge into the frigid, stormy waters, Clarence, the angel sent from heaven to save George to earn his wings, intervenes. Clarence jumps into the frigid night water before George can jump, and George's caring nature kicks in and saves Clarence.

George tells Clarence that it would have been better if he were never born. This gives Clarence the idea to show George what the world would look like without him in it. It doesn't take long to see the amazing impact one person had on his family, friends, and community and how the world was much better off *with* George Bailey in it. After seeing just how foolish his thoughts about suicide were, George races home to be embraced by his family, friends, and community.

Even though everyone's heart goes out to George Bailey, the real hero of the story is Clarence. You see, Clarence gives George a powerful gift: to see the world without him in it. You do the very same thing every day with your clients. You have conversations with them, showing them at some point that they will not be in this world, and just how will that world look? Will it be a world of friends and family thankful for the planning and foresight that was done that allowed their world to stay intact? Will it be a world in which the legacy left will be one of love, thoughtfulness, selflessness, and dignity? When an advisor is involved, this is always the case. This is our obligation and commitment, and it's why we chose this wonderful calling of ours. Each one of you is Clarence, and you have a gift to give to your clients—to help them identify, plan, and reach those important milestones in their lifetime. We must also show them what the world will look like if they are not there and enable them to be prepared so that their vision and wishes of what they want to occur can come to fruition.

> Clarence gives George a powerful gift: to see the world without him in it. You do the very same thing every day with your clients.

As an advisor, you are one of the angels among us. You are "others-focused." You truly live a wonderful life dedicated to serving others so they also can live wonderful lives.

Let's help as many people as we can. Let's earn our wings.

This chapter was inspired by former GAMA President R. Michael Condrey, CFP®, CLU®, ChFC®, CASL®, in his keynote presentation at LAMP 1998.

CHAPTER 9

ADVISORS ARE THE FLYWHEELS WHO HELP CLIENTS TAKE ACTION

A financial advisor encourages clients to *start and stay the course* **to financial security for themselves and the next generation.**

Advisors need to understand the psychology and general mind-set about most people. Almost every prospective client or prospect you will encounter has good intentions. They have intentions of providing for, protecting, planning for, and being responsible for their own future and their family's future. Rarely will someone disagree fundamentally with what you are trying to help them with:

1. Having proper risk-management strategies and products in place so that they're ready if and when the uncertainties of life occur

2. Accumulating sufficient funds and having a wealth-distribution strategy in place to ensure that they do not outlive their money and can leave a legacy

But because of human nature, there are two reasons most people don't take action in these areas:

1. A sense of urgency rarely exists about acting on those intentions *today*. By nature, all of us are procrastinators—not necessarily because we are lazy, but because we believe we have plenty of time and will do it at some point in the future.

2. Most people think the "uncertainties of life" occur with *other* people—never with them. *Other* people become disabled, and *other* people die prematurely. Those things simply won't happen to *me*. We have been hardwired to think we are immune to these unfortunate realities.

So, when you combine a lack of urgency with denial, it is not surprising that people often postpone meetings and say they need to "think about it." They do not typically wake up on a Saturday morning with the plan for the day being to interview and select the appropriate financial advisor to steer their course to financial security.

> When you combine a lack of urgency with denial, it is not surprising that people often postpone meetings and say they need to "think about it."

The solution is that when we, as advisors, serve as a flywheel to help clients take action. Here is the definition of a flywheel: "A heavy revolving wheel in a machine that is used to increase the machine's momentum and thereby provide greater stability or a reserve of available power during interruptions in the delivery of power to the machine."

In our business, the way this flywheel gets started is by an advisor knowing that people left to their own devices will not initiate the conversation. The flywheel starts by the *advisor* initiating contact with the client. Like football, dancing, wrestling, and tennis, financial advising is also a contact sport—when you make contact, you win!

As you review your clients' plans and goals, it is a good time to make sure that human life value amounts of insurance are in place and that you consider both term and permanent insurance needs. We know that is the only kind guaranteed to pay. As you catch up and visit with your clients about their children, insist that if they are adult children, they need to meet you so you can talk with them about their own needs. If you partner with a junior advisor, he or she can do so.

Most of all, take a few minutes and remind them what it is you really do—you help them start and stay the course to financial security by educating, motivating, and inspiring them to take action on all of those important goals and milestones they want to accomplish in this lifetime and beyond.

This isn't and never will be about beating the indexes each year or managing assets for 25 basis points.

This isn't about ROI but about ROL (Return on Life), and that is what you do—you are their life planner.

Intentions are worthless; action matters! As a financial advisor, you are the vehicle, the very mechanism—the flywheel—required to have every one of those well-thought-out goals and plans to come to fruition. You do not manage clients' money; you manage their *behavior.* You are in the habit-formation and behavior-modification business.

Without your leadership, compassion, conviction, and determination, your clients won't stand a fighting chance either starting or staying the course without you. Denial and procrastination will win them over. Don't ever get caught commoditizing yourself by being viewed purely as a manager of assets. Stand tall and take pride in knowing that you are *changing lives, forever*—one life, one client at a time. It all starts with *you!*

EMOTION

LOGIC

YOU DO NOT MANAGE CLIENTS' MONEY; YOU MANAGE THEIR
BEHAVIOR. YOU ARE IN THE HABIT-FORMATION AND
BEHAVIOR-MODIFICATION BUSINESS.

HOPE

CHAPTER 10

ADVISORS HELP PEOPLE WHO CAN NEVER REPAY THEM

We like to repeat a quote often stated by Lewis Katz: "It's never a perfect day unless you help someone who can never hope to repay you."[6]

The moment you ensure that a client's risk is covered is the moment he or she will place you in the coveted position of being someone who makes a difference in his or her life and future. Your clients will not be able to imagine their lives without you.

Regardless of the amount you earned on the implementation of a client's life insurance program—and for that matter, all the compensation you have received while serving as that client's advisor—you have done infinitely more good for the client and his or her family's future than any dollar amount the client has paid you or a carrier. Every day, you have the ability to place life insurance for clients, and they will never be able to repay you. Please take a moment to embrace and accept that. It is the irrefutable truth.

Insurance companies create the products, and in doing so, *protect people*. As advisors, we *help people build hopes and dreams*. It is your intervention that initiates the conversations around what their vision of the future will look like. You are the one who helps them understand what this world will look like one day when they are no longer in it. You are the one who helps them build a path to make sure they accomplish the most important hopes and dreams they have:

> As advisors, we help people build hopes and dreams.

- Providing an education for their children

- Gifting money to their grandchildren, charities, and important causes

- Helping children pay for weddings

- Passing businesses to the next generation

- Having the resources to ensure that they do not outlive their money

- Leaving a legacy of significance

Before you come into the picture, having all of that protection is merely a hope and a dream for people, but far from reality. What you bring to the table is *implementation*. After you help them build their life plan and implement the proper habits, strategies, mind-set, and products, the insurance companies take over as the protectors of those very hopes and dreams. Insurance companies protect people; you make their hopes and dreams a reality. That is priceless—and there is no way they could ever repay you for such valuable support and guidance. That is what makes it so rewarding.

---

6. Lewis Katz was an entrepreneur, philanthropist, and beloved Temple University graduate, trustee, and advocate. He once was a co-owner of the New Jersey Nets and Devils. On May 15, 2014, Katz delivered a motivational commencement speech to the graduating class of his alma mater, Temple University. Just sixteen days later, he died in a plane crash. The North American Association of Commencement Officers (NAACO) posthumously named Katz the best commencement speaker of 2014. The Temple University School of Medicine was renamed the Lewis Katz School of Medicine School on October 13, 2015.

CHAPTER 11
OUR INDUSTRY NEEDS MORE ADVISORS

In 2003, something very good happened within our firm: we established our Servant Leadership Committee based on Jim Collins's Mars Team concept. A Mars Team is the handful of people you would take with you if you had to replicate your business on Mars. Our group got together and had a breakthrough strategy meeting. We figured out our *why*—the reason our group wakes up each day and puts the uniform on, if you will, and goes out to the battlefield to fight the good fight.

We figured out our why and captured it in three simple words: changing lives, forever.

What we discovered that day was our firm's purpose. First and foremost, we exist to change the lives of the advisors we give the opportunity to enter this wonderful calling of ours. We want to find talented people who want to have a career that provides the three I's: impact, independence, and income. We want to give them the chance to be in business *for* themselves but never *by* themselves. We want to help them build world-class financial planning practices where the foundation is risk management and protection—insurance—*first*.

RECRUITING ADVISORS TO SHARE THE MIRACLE OF LIFE INSURANCE

We decided that day that if our organization were to do only one thing, it would be to recruit, find, grow, and develop financial advisors who would spread the good news of the Miracle of Life Insurance, and in turn, fulfill our vision of changing their clients' lives, forever. As our firm changes the lives of the advisors we bring into this wonderful calling of ours, they, in turn, change the lives of their clients forever by helping them start and stay the course to financial security and protecting them from the many uncertainties of life.

Each time we hire a new advisor, we change the life of the twenty-two-year-old recent college grad as he or she builds a career that is virtually unparalleled in terms of impact and opportunity. Our advisors change the lives of hundreds and perhaps thousands of clients' lives over their entire career.

When we think about the ripple effect or the butterfly effect, we cannot help but smile and think that the one God-given life we have been blessed to receive is being well spent, with countless lives being impacted as a result of the good works of every advisor we recruit and train.

> When we think about the ripple effect or the butterfly effect, we cannot help but smile and think that the one God-given life we have been blessed to receive is being well spent, with countless lives being impacted as a result of the good works of every advisor we recruit and train.

THE SUPPLY AND DEMAND ASPECT OF THIS CAREER

When we interview candidates for the advisor career, we educate them about the "supply and demand" phenomenon that is occurring in our industry.

First, in terms of supply, we have a dwindling number of advisors to serve our burgeoning population. In 1998, our primary industry association, the National Association of Insurance and Financial Advisors (NAIFA), had more than 104,000 members. Today that number is under 50,000. We could write a doctoral thesis about the benefits NAIFA provides all of us and our clients.

Our supply of advisors is low and decreasing.

Also, the average age of our practicing advisors ranges from fifty-two to fifty-seven years old. This tells us that in the next decade, we will have even fewer advisors to serve the public because many will begin to phase out of their practices and retire. The bottom line is that our supply of advisors is low and decreasing.

When we hear statistics of an industry in which the average age of producers and leaders is the mid- to late fifties, we look in the mirror and see the future of our industry. North Star makes a very deliberate choice each day to focus on recruiting inexperienced advisors, with an emphasis on college recruiting, which we believe is required to secure our industry's future. We want to embrace the genius of the "and" and not only grow our firm with each new hire, but add another person to the ranks who serves in the general public each day, helping so many people start and stay the course to financial security. There simply are not enough of us.

If we all collectively keep hiring new people into our wonderful career, we all win—firms, home offices, advisors, and mostly our clients, future clients, and communities.

As for demand, our society has an increasing need and demand for insurance because people are living longer than ever before. The first person who might live to be 150 years old has been born already. With advances in medicine, nutrition, fitness, and so many related areas, our life spans are increasing at record rates. Compound that with the massive financial illiteracy that our country suffers. A recent industry study indicated that more than 40 percent of the population would give themselves a grade of D or F in the area of financial literacy. People tend to know *what* to do when it comes to the basics of financial planning—spend less than you earn, save for the future, and insure yourself properly—but few actually do those things.

YOYO
You're On Your Own!

The last few generations have seen a shift of responsibility in providing for people's futures. At one time, employers and our government played a huge part in helping people have money for the future, through pensions and Social Security. But today, as industry consultant Nick Murray says, it's YOYO—"You're on your own!"

Individuals are now responsible for making sure they do not outlive their money. As more and more financial information bombards us every day through the media and the Internet, the general public is looking for those who can provide answers and wisdom. The demand and need for our services has never been more warranted. Without the guidance and counsel that you, as an advisor, bring to the relationship with clients, they will not be prepared for the future or the uncertainties of life that are always among us. You are the one who helps them form the proper financial habits, serves as a behavior manager, and makes sure they do not become their own worst enemy and fall into the trap of buying high and selling low. Heaven knows your clients will rationalize to themselves a lower amount of insurance than what they truly need.

We need more advisors than ever who can help educate, motivate, and guide people to make sound financial decisions.

> Your clients will rationalize to themselves a lower amount of insurance than what they truly need.

CHAPTER 12

IT TAKES A PERSON OF CHARACTER TO BUY INSURANCE

Insurance is a selfless gift, a gift of love. Those who buy it are people with integrity and character. And those who dedicate a life's calling to it are selfless people with integrity and character. They live our vision of changing lives, forever, and believe in our values of responsibility, faith, integrity, growth, gratitude, and service (RFIGGS).

Life insurance is so deeply steeped into our firm that we believe even if it were not profitable for us to sell, we would manage to find other profit centers within the firm to make sure we would dedicate the time and resources required to implement the Miracle of Life Insurance for people. We really do not have a choice because life insurance is not just a product; it is *who we are.*

> **Life insurance is not just a product; it is who we are.**

A SERIOUS RESPONSIBILITY

This book is dedicated to the dignity of the product of life insurance and to the people of character who purchase and sell it.

As humans, we are hardwired to resist thinking about a future without ourselves in it. We are not inclined to think that way, and doing so can be uncomfortable. It's natural, so don't get frustrated about it; just accept it. Try to think about the situation from a practical perspective and examine why every family needs life insurance.

We take on numerous responsibilities during a lifetime: completing an education, getting married, having children, launching and running a business, and giving back to our communities. We feel responsible and obligated to the people and entities in our lives. Buying life insurance is another important responsibility we need to take care of—before we have medical conditions that could prevent us from securing it.

We demonstrate gratitude by being responsible with whatever it is we are grateful for. That is the ultimate characteristic of being responsible. If you are really grateful for your family and the other people and organizations that have made you who you are, then demonstrate being grateful by acting responsibly toward them. One way to show gratitude, responsibility, and character is to own the proper amount of life insurance—enough to cover your human life value—so that those people and things can continue on without your involvement and dedication.

It takes a person of character to purchase life insurance because it really is a selfless product. You are not going to enjoy the benefits of life insurance; your loved ones are. You will never, ever see a penny of that death benefit. You will be gone. It takes character to recognize that and follow through on it.

> **You are not going to enjoy the benefits of life insurance; your loved ones are.**

For the same reasons, it takes a financial advisor with integrity to bring up this difficult subject—people's mortality.

LIFE INSURANCE IS LOVE

Years ago, the Life Happens organization produced a beautiful poem that we display prominently in our office:

Because he loved me,
He did the dishes,
Rubbed my feet,
Surprised me with tulips,
Took me to musicals even though he didn't like them,
Carried my bags while I did the shopping,
Held my hand.

He died of cancer four years ago.

Because he loved me,
I can stay in our home.
I can be there for our children.
I can afford to pay their college education.
I can worry about the other things in life besides money.

He still loves me,
And he still shows it.

Before she retired in 2013, Nancy Mullen had been a Securian team member for fifteen years. She started in the insurance industry in 1971. She shared the following personal story with us right before she retired. It demonstrates in a compelling way that life insurance equals love:

Every time I go to one of your winter or summer meetings, I love the Real Life Stories. I've often wanted to share this story of mine with you. Since I am retiring in the fall, I thought I had better send to you now or never.

I was raised by a single mom, and we lived with my grandparents, who were from Sicily. We lived in Pittsburgh, Pennsylvania. My mom and aunt both worked, so my cousin and I were with our grandparents every day. Fairly frequently, my grandmother had a visit from the "John Hancock Man."

He had a large book he would open on his knees, and when he called my cousin's name and my name, my grandmother would go into her apron pocket and hand him money. He would write something in his book and in a little ledger she kept. My cousin and I thought this was pretty interesting, so one day we asked him why our grandmother gave him money when he said our names. He said, "Because your grandmother loves you very much and wants you to be happy." We were four or five, so I guess that answer was as good as any.

My grandmother died right before my eighteenth birthday, and the John

54

Hancock Man was at her funeral. He came up to my cousin and said, "Remember me and my answer about how much your grandma loved you?" He told us that because of the money she gave him, he would be sending us each a check with our grandma's love and hope that we would use it wisely and be happy. The checks arrived and in 1966 paid for a considerable amount of our college tuition.

The John Hancock Man told us that our grandmother was a center of influence for him. She could read and write, so when friends and neighbors wanted letters read or sent to Italy, they would take them to my grandmother. She knew everyone who was getting married and having babies, and she would let him know.

At the time, John Hancock Co. would give little silver spoons to new moms for their babies. He would take the spoon over to the new parents and say, "Mary Licata wanted you to have this and for me to introduce myself to you."

I always think about this and my grandmother when I hear the Real Life Stories and keep thinking I would relay it to you someday. I finally got around to doing it. Because of her, I've always associated insurance with love—I guess that's why I've made it my career.

Thanks.

Nancy A. Mullen
Senior Compliance Analyst
Securian Financial Services Inc.

CHAPTER 13

TRUE STORIES ABOUT LIFE INSURANCE MIRACLES FROM NORTH STAR RESOURCE GROUP ADVISORS

To demonstrate the miracle of life insurance and the way it has protected the financial future of families across America, we are including stories from some of our advisors and managers.

You will notice a common theme among some of these stories: the prospect in many cases did not want to buy life insurance—at least not right then. But the advisors urged them to go through with it, and that difficult prodding resulted in a secure financial future for the families.

Ryan Anderson, CFP®
Financial Advisor, North Star Resource Group

I was referred to Kirstin by the wife of my good friend, Jon, when she was still single. In fact, I was the best man and she was the maid of honor in the couple's wedding. She had met her husband, Alan, and gotten married shortly after that. Over the years, they had three beautiful daughters.

Alan was a great guy, and in our annual reviews, he would ask me more questions about how I was doing than I could possibly ask him. He was a hard-working guy who loved his family but had demons that none of us could see. In our review in the spring of 2012, we decided to restructure their insurance (now having their third daughter) and add some coverage. He mentioned that they had a higher-than-normal credit-card bill and wanted to hold off until the summer or fall to increase the coverage.

One fall Saturday in 2012, Jon called me and asked if he could stop by. I figured it was because my wife and I had just moved into a new home and had our first daughter. When he got there, I could tell something was up. He asked if he could talk to me alone in the other room. I'll never forget that feeling when he said, "Alan killed himself." I was in shock. He had been depressed for years, and I had no idea. I had seen him a few months before, and we had great talks and laughed a lot. I couldn't imagine how this was possible.

After Jon left, the wheels started turning. I immediately logged in to SecurianAdvisor to see how much coverage Alan had. It was a sizable amount, but I was still nervous and worried if it was enough. For those of you who have never paid a claim, these are the thoughts that go through your head for your first claim. Yep, thirteen years in the business, and I had never paid a claim.

Kirstin came in weeks later after gathering the necessary information from Alan's employer and other sources. He only had $10,000 in insurance through work. We talked about Alan and laughed and cried. Then came the numbers talk. How much was there? The total was $625,000. We were able to turn that into a stream

> We were able to turn that into a stream of income for her with very little risk. It has allowed her to quit her job as a financial analyst and spend more time with the three girls, who were all under five at the time of Alan's death.

of income for her with very little risk. It has allowed her to quit her job as a financial analyst and spend more time with the three girls, who were all under five at the time of Alan's death.

Kirstin says she'll eventually go back to work, but this money has given her the ability to not be forced into anything. She has been able to stay in the house, keep the girls in the same school systems, and volunteer a lot of her time because she isn't currently working.

Todd Bramson, CFP®, CLU, ChFC, CFS
Senior Partner, North Star Resource Group

As a nineteen-year-old college student, I became licensed as a college agent with Northwestern Mutual life in their internship program. This, coupled with my marketing and risk/insurance degree from the University of Wisconsin, was a valuable starting point to my business career.

The very first life insurance policy I sold (besides the one I purchased for myself) was to my college roommate, Bob. Locking in a basic plan, securing the additional purchase benefit, and using this as a cornerstone of his long-term financial security was the motivation. Because he attended college on a full-ride scholarship, he had a few extra dollars to plan for his future.

In a complete and unexpected surprise turn of events, only months after buying the policy, Bob was diagnosed with cancer. After a hard-fought but short battle, he died. The policy he had purchased for his long-term financial security, for retirement savings, to protect him and his future wife and kids, paid off a death benefit when he was only twenty years old!

> **The proceeds helped his parents replenish their savings account, which was drained because of all the time they took off from work to be with Bob during his illness.**

I delivered a $50,000 check to his parents in a very emotional meeting. They didn't even know he had the policy. The proceeds helped his parents replenish their savings account, which was drained because of all the time they took off from work to be with Bob during his illness. Some of the proceeds helped pay for his sister's wedding. More went to his younger brother's college education.

This situation inspired me to go into the insurance and financial planning field. I pledged to make sure that this experience would help me help many others during my career. Bob's unselfish act of purchasing life insurance at a young age has had a ripple effect that went beyond the significant financial benefit for his immediate family.

Joseph P. Fox, CLU, ChFC, CLTC
Senior Partner, North Star Resource Group

When Greg and Melissa Knoll were only in their mid-twenties, they met with me to discuss their financial future. They were young and healthy and didn't expect to need life insurance soon. But they had a new home with a mortgage and were ready to start a family. Greg already had the maximum amount of coverage he could get from his employer but knew he needed more and bought it through me.

In 2006, when Greg was thirty-six, he began having chronic heartburn that wouldn't go away. After gallbladder surgery failed to cure it, doctors discovered a rare form of stomach cancer. Greg passed away two years later.

The life insurance proceeds paid off a lot of debt that had accumulated during Greg's illness. They also allowed Melissa to pay off her mortgage and set up college funds for her two young daughters.

I don't think any of us can quite comprehend what goes through a person's mind at that point when she realizes that her husband isn't going to be there anymore, and financially it is all on her shoulders.

At Greg's wake, Melissa's mother pulled me aside and asked, "Is everything going to be okay? Are they going to lose the house?" I assured her that because of Greg and Melissa's wise planning, they would be just fine. She needed to hear that. At a time when so much else was going on, I don't think they really knew the details about what insurance they had or if it would be enough. You know, a person can't quite put her mind around it at that point. So not only does the life insurance have to be in place, but I think a family needs someone in the advisor role who can convey to them that they have done the right things, and everything is going to be okay.

When I got into this business twenty-five years ago, life insurance was the lead product. So I was trained to lead client discussions with life insurance. And, while North Star Resource Group does more investment business than it used to, that certainly is not at the expense of our life insurance business.

I think many companies and advisors have moved their focus from life insurance to investment products because it is the path of least resistance. What I mean by that is that it is difficult to sell life insurance. Nobody wants to face the reality of their own mortality. It is one of the same reasons that people don't draft wills—they don't want to face some of those issues. In a fee-based plan, there is often a section that specifies the client's life insurance need and recommends what should be implemented. But it really takes somebody with enough conviction to put the right plan together. The right plan is a needs-based plan that can be described as a pyramid. The base of that pyramid

> The right plan is a needs-based plan that can be described as a pyramid. The base of that pyramid has to be risk management—insurance.

has to be risk management—insurance. It has to specify what will happen in the event of death or what happens in the event of disability. If we haven't covered those areas first, there is absolutely no sense in moving on beyond that because you have built your plan on a base of sand. I don't know that everybody has the conviction to do that, but that is the only way to build a properly designed needs-based financial plan.

I really think that our mission as advisors is to protect the hopes and dreams of our clients. What we sell to our clients is a promise to pay when they need it most. There is no other product that can do that other than life insurance. There was no investment program that I could have put together that accomplished what we accomplished for the Knoll family, or any family for that matter, other than life insurance. That is why it has to be at the core of any plan; otherwise, the plan could easily get derailed.

In my twenty years in this business, I've learned lots of things. But this may be the most important lesson of all.

In my business, it's easy to get caught up in illustrations, charts and graphs, rates of return, and product features. But I've learned that our business really isn't about those things at all. My mission is to protect the hopes and dreams of our clients. What I sell to my clients is a promise to pay when they need it most.

In my industry:

- We keep families in their homes.
- We keep businesses in business.
- We keep hopes and dreams alive.

Advisors often think it's a big deal whether we sell term, whole life, or universal life. When the worst happens, our clients don't care what kind of insurance it was. They just want to know, "Do I have enough? Will everything be all right?"

As difficult and as tragic as Greg's death was, I'm glad that I had satisfactory answers to those questions. For the girls, I can't replace their dad or his presence at their college graduation ceremony or his ability to walk them down the aisle when they get married. But from a financial standpoint, I can make sure that they can afford to attend the college of their choice and have the wedding of their dreams.

Of course, none of what I've been able to do for the Knoll family would have been possible without Greg and Melissa's high level of responsibility. I give them a lot of credit for protecting their hopes and dreams at such a young age. Greg and Melissa first bought life insurance from me in their mid-twenties. A lot of people their age would have put off the decision to purchase life insurance until later in life, if at all.

> Had Greg waited until his mid-thirties— still young by most people's standards— he would have been uninsurable.

Had Greg waited until his mid-thirties—still young by most people's standards—he would have been uninsurable.

Greg lived life to the fullest. He left a desk job to become an undercover police officer and SWAT team member. He liked guns, adventure, fast cars, fast boats, and snowmobiles. But even when he was living at a faster pace than the rest of us, Greg was never reckless. He couldn't afford to be. He had a family to provide for. He exercised the same caution in the financial plans we put together for his family. And because of it, I'm happy to say that Melissa and the girls are financially secure.

CR&O

In 2009, Joe received top honors from the life insurance industry when he was named a recipient of the realLIFEstories Client Service Award from the nonprofit organization LIFE Foundation*, now known as Life Happens. The award recognizes insurance professionals for their outstanding service to a family or individual.

Joe and his client, Melissa Knoll, were honored at a convention of the National Association of Insurance and Financial Advisors (NAIFA), and their story appeared in the September 14, 2009, issue of *Newsweek*. To view the video that Life Happens created about Melissa's story, go to http://www.northstarfinancial.com/find_an_ advisor/joseph-fox.

Below, Melissa describes the situation from her perspective. Her daughters are seventeen and twelve now. She often speaks to groups, including many insurance companies, at the request of the Life Happens organization about the importance of life insurance.

Melissa Knoll, Client of Joe Fox

I think people's reluctance to buy life insurance is a combination of many different things. First, I think the people who are stretched very thin, income-wise, are probably the people who need it most—parents. They are so busy living day to day and paying for all of the family's daily necessities that I don't think they have the time to thoughtfully plan or think about an expense like life insurance. I know from my own experience as a really busy parent that you never feel like you have extra money. I think people have good intentions, and in general, they think life insurance is a good idea, but they don't actually have the time or the perceived extra money to sit down and actually purchase life insurance—to care for their family in that way.

We met Joe Fox through a man named Tony, who had been working as a salesperson for a local snowmobile dealership. My husband, Greg, had purchased a snowmobile from Tony. Then Tony changed careers and started working at North Star; Joe was his mentor. Tony worked kind of under Joe, and he asked us to come in and talk about our financial future.

We were so busy. I remember that it was really difficult to figure out when we could both get the time off of work and have the kids taken care of and get in to see them. We talked about life insurance as well as setting aside money for our daughter to go to college. They recommended that we put away about $450 a month, but we could not afford that. There was no way, so Greg asked him instead what he thought about trading up to a 4-stroke Ski-Doo snowmobile.

I think one of the most important things to realize is that people have the misconception that they can't afford life insurance. Also, sometimes people are a little reluctant or embarrassed about their debt or the way they spend money. This is true even of people who are extremely successful or have very high salaries.

Even many of them probably feel vulnerable talking to somebody about finances, thinking that the advisor is going to be judgmental about how they are spending their money. But that couldn't have been further from the truth for us.

I was a little intimidated thinking about what they might to talk to us about because we didn't have anything. We were young and had just bought a house. We really didn't, in my eyes, have much to be going to a financial planner for. But Joe worked with us and met with us each year. He would give us recommendations and say, "Here are the areas where you are not really covered. This is where you are not where I would like to see you." Then Greg and I would look at it and agree that maybe we could manage $2,000 for the year, so we would put that money toward one of Joe's recommendations. Then we would get a raise or a bonus and meet with Joe. We would tell him, "Okay, now we have five thousand dollars to work with, but we want to go on a trip. So really, we have two thousand dollars to work with. Where should that go?"

When Greg got sick, we spent two years barely getting by. Things were really hard when he was going through treatment and wasn't working overtime at his full-time job or working at his part-time job. We also had lots of expenses. We basically survived on donations from family, friends, and our parents. It kind of sounds crazy, but I really didn't know what was available in terms of our life insurance. We had focused so much on trying to get him well and trying to beat the cancer that I never looked at the life insurance or asked myself, "What if something happened to him?" He and I never talked about it—the "what if." For us, and probably for most people, that is why I didn't even want to think about that because that would have put it into our minds that he wasn't going to make it. We always just focused on him surviving.

So when Joe told us we were going to be okay financially, it was an absolute relief, but I would not say that it even felt like good news at that time.

I recently saw some of my friends, and I said, "It is so important to get life insurance." I asked them if they had life insurance on their kids, and there are a good number who do not. I have life insurance on my kids. It is not so much because I want to insure them or to have money for funeral expenses or something if they were to die. It is so that I can preserve their insurability. So my children have insurance policies. That will guarantee them the possibility of increasing their

I have life insurance on my kids so that I can preserve their insurability.

coverage and having life insurance moving forward when they are adults, without ever having to have a medical exam.

Some of my friends didn't even think about that. Most people don't know that. You think life insurance is to provide money when somebody dies, but really I consider it an investment and protection for the future for my kids. And for myself. My brother had surgery when he was nineteen years old for a congenital heart defect. As a result, he is not eligible for life insurance. There are a lot of people who won't be eligible for life insurance if a medical issue arises in their thirties or forties. The time to get it is when you are young and you have no health concerns.

When I started speaking to the insurance groups, it came as a surprise to me that some advisors are hesitant to sell life insurance. My friends who have candle parties and bag parties are constantly telling me all about what they sell and what they do. I realized it is very tragic that people who have really valuable, critical information about life insurance—agents and advisors—are shy about sharing it. They hesitate to share this critical information with their friends, their family members, and the parents of their kids' friends.

> When I started speaking to the insurance groups, it came as a surprise to me that some advisors are hesitant to sell life insurance.

In doing these talks throughout the country, I have had the opportunity to hear and talk with some motivational speakers. I realized that they always ask for an action item. They always tell the people in the audience that they want them to do something specific. So I created my own action item.

Now I tell advisors, "Be bold. You are the ones who have the valuable information that can make the difference in a family's life and help them achieve their hopes and their dreams."

In the end, the best surgeons and best oncologists in the country weren't able to save Greg. But life insurance was able to preserve his dreams for his kids.

*(Working with this individual or firm is not a guarantee of future financial results. Investors should conduct their own evaluation.)

Marshall W. Gifford, CLU, ChFC
Senior Partner, North Star Resource Group

Marshall became an advisor for North Star Resource Group in 1993. He began working with the dental marketplace right away. Less than two years later, he began working with physicians too because one of his dentist clients was married to a physician. He used an educational approach, offering to help dentists and physicians who were just graduating from dental school and medical school and beginning their practices. He also made presentations about financial planning to the student dental association.

Here are two stories from Marshall about the impact life insurance makes in people's lives. His third story is about a client who never completed his applications for life insurance, and his wife suffered financially after his unexpected death.

Insurance Written Just in Time

Back in 2002, I met with a couple who were about thirty years old. The husband was just finishing his medical residency. They had a young child, and his wife was pregnant with their second child. We were talking about the normal financial topics, and I kind of pushed them to make sure they got their life insurance squared away, even though it was a little bit more than he wanted to pay during the transition that summer from his residency to his practice. He hadn't started earning a full income yet. When I showed him what his monthly premium would be, he said, "I will do it once I start making money."

I don't know why I was fairly blunt, but I told him, "No, that doesn't make any sense. Just write the check and get it done. You are not going to miss the eighty dollars."

They bought life insurance in late August, and about four weeks after we got the policy enforced, he started feeling badly. He found out that he had lung cancer.

I had a lot of correspondence with the two of them, and they updated me on his health. Finally, his disease progressed to the point where his doctors decided to give him only palliative care. They were not trying to cure him anymore but just keep him alive a little bit longer so that he could see his second child be born. He died about two months after the baby was born, the next May.

> The whole point of the meeting was for him to cross off as much as possible and enjoy the last couple weeks of his life, knowing that he left his family and his two kids in a pretty decent financial spot.

About a month before he died, I met with him and his wife. The focus of the meeting was that he wanted to be at peace financially. He was dying, and he just wanted to have one less thing to worry about. So the whole point of the meeting was for him to cross off as much as possible and enjoy the last couple weeks of his life, knowing that he left his family and his two kids in a pretty decent financial spot.

I went to the funeral and met his whole family. They gave me big hugs and even cried a little bit. They told me how thankful they were for the work that we had done and said that having everything in order financially was one big burden the family didn't have to think about. It was a pretty emotional process.

A Casualty of Cancer at Age Thirty-Seven

I run a very successful practice, and I really don't have to add any new clients at this point if I don't want to. But I still feel compelled to meet new people and to get out there and educate people. Shaun McDuffee and I opened an office in Chicago in 2005. We hosted an event in downtown Chicago for practicing physicians. We invited practicing physicians to a dinner discussion where we talked about key financial issues that they face. It was the first event we hosted in Chicago, and it was at Northwestern University Hospital.

One of the physicians who attended with his wife became a client of ours, and we wrote life insurance on him. Over the next three years, they had some difficulties having children, so they were adopting a child from Latin America. While they were down there, he started to feel sick. When he came home, he was diagnosed with esophageal cancer, and he died a year later. He was thirty-seven.

I think about that. Had we decided not to continue to expand the practice and conduct educational events to reach people, his wife's life and their daughter's life would be significantly different than it is today. She recently remarried. I still have a good relationship with her and still manage all of her money for her and new family.

> Had we decided not to continue to expand the practice and conduct educational events to reach people, his wife's life and their daughter's life would be significantly different than it is today.

It is heartbreaking to watch someone wither away to nothing from lung cancer or esophageal cancer. People who go through an illness like that have a lot of time to think and dwell on whether they did what they should have while they were alive and whether their family is going to be in good financial shape or not.

That is one of those stories that shows what happens when someone is smart enough to get life insurance in place early on. People who do that are people of character who are demonstrating the greatest act of love possible for their loved ones. They are making a promise to protect their loved ones' future. Unfortunately, some people don't follow through, and the result is disastrous.

The Blank Application, Still on His Desk

I once worked with a dentist in South Dakota who was young—in his late twenties. We sent him applications but didn't hear back from him. We kept following up and asking, "Hey, can you get those back to us? Please complete the applications and get them back to us."

We followed up every couple of weeks for several months. But he never completed the application. One night, he went to work out at the gym, then got home and was watching the news with his wife. When he stood up to go to bed, he keeled over and died of a massive heart attack.

His wife called me and told me that he had passed away. She said, "I told him so many times to sign that application. It is sitting right in the spot where he does all of his paperwork right now. I am so mad at him. I will never forgive him for that."

Jeffrey K. Jarnes, CFP®, CLU, ChFC, RHU
Financial Advisor, North Star Resource Group

Early in my thirty-six-year career, I began working with a client named John Hulsby. He and his wife, Louise, lived in Minneapolis. John was a thirty-year veteran employee at Honeywell. He was an interesting guy who worked his way up the corporate ladder. Through his hard work and commitment to the company, he was making a healthy six-figure income by the time he retired at age sixty-two. John was proud of his career, his healthy Honeywell pension plan, and most importantly, his five grandchildren.

A year before John retired, we scheduled a review meeting to update his overall financial plan. Because John was very healthy for his age, our "pension maximization analysis" software strongly supported my recommendation to elect the "life only" option on his Honeywell pension plan. Although this choice meant that John would need to secure private life insurance to protect Louise in the event of his early demise, this option would allow them to receive about $8,000 per month for the remainder of John's life.

Retirees usually elect the "joint and 100 percent survivor" option to ensure that pension payments will continue to the surviving spouse. But, in John's case, the cost of taking that election meant a lifelong reduction of $1,600 per month to his $8,000 pension payment, which would permanently lower their income to $6,400 per month. Over the course of his normal life expectancy, this would amount to a great deal of lost income during his retirement years.

One of John's retirement ambitions was to create and manage a real estate development company. Soon he purchased a parcel of land near his home, in the outskirts of Minneapolis. His ultimate goal was to develop the land into an executive golf course surrounded by a neighborhood of modestly priced homes.

Over the next couple of years, John's real estate expertise proved to be far inferior to the engineering skills that he left behind at Honeywell. The development project ran into the usual delays and problems, which put a constant drain on John's retirement assets. As the real estate market continued to sour, the investments that John and Louise had set aside for their golden years were soon depleted. In an act of desperation, John had to "fire-sale" the failing project, and the end result was devastating; except for John's ongoing pension income, they were broke.

As if John's financial troubles weren't bad enough, he then developed an unexpected health problem. One morning he woke up and noticed that his skin was a bit jaundiced, so he went to see his family doctor for an evaluation. The next few days turned out to be the worst days of his life as he was diagnosed with pancreatic cancer. The condition was inoperable, and John's oncologist told him that he had less than eighteen months to live. Now, not only were their finances in big trouble, but his Honeywell pension payments would stop, and other than the life insurance proceeds, no other assets were available for Louise.

> In an act of desperation, John had to "fire-sale" the failing project, and the end result was devastating; except for John's ongoing pension income, they were broke.

Fortunately, the private life insurance we had put in place to secure the risk of John's life-only pension decision was there. In fact, not only would those tax-free benefits be made available to Louise immediately upon John's death, but there was another provision I had heard about, but never used, known as the "critical illness" benefit.

(Additional costs and restrictions apply. Distributions under this agreement, as with any policy loans or withdrawals, may create an adverse tax result in the event of a lapse or policy surrender and will reduce both the cash value and death benefit.)

The specific critical illness rider on John's life insurance policy would allow him to withdraw a substantial amount of the death benefit *during* his lifetime because of the terminal illness (defined as a prognosis of two years or less). I discussed this feature with John and Louise, and immediately, I could see that a heavy burden had been lifted from each of them. Now they would be able to redeem some of John's death benefit (during his short remaining life span), which would give them the funds they needed to get their affairs in order, clean up their remaining debts, and do something they never thought possible: create one last quality experience with their five grandchildren by taking them to Disney World.

> The critical illness rider on John's life insurance policy would allow him to withdraw a substantial amount of the death benefit during his lifetime because of the terminal illness.

Over the next few days, we worked on the paperwork for the critical-illness payment and were able to plan properly for Louise's continuing financial stability. Shortly thereafter, John received a check for a substantial amount of money as part of his "critical illness" benefit, and they worked with a travel agent to finalize the details of their trip.

This incredible benefit was going to allow them to take their five grandchildren to Disney World and create memories that those grandchildren would never forget!

I met with John and Louise after their trip, and they said it was the vacation of a lifetime. The grandchildren had a terrific experience and will always cherish the great memory that Grandma and Grandpa created for them.

Four months after the trip to Disney World, John died. His pancreatic cancer was extremely aggressive, and the final weeks of his life were miserable. However, the celebration of John's life was remarkable. The oldest grandchild spoke about the wonderful trip they had just shared with "Grampy." It was a tear-jerking salute, and it hardened my commitment to the life insurance industry and to the importance of that amazing product.

Louise is still a client of mine, and the balance of the life insurance proceeds have been invested in a conservative portfolio for over three decades. Those funds have comfortably supported her lifestyle. Once again, it is a testimony to the financial planning industry and to the advice we provide to our clients.

This story has a lot of twists and turns, but it exemplifies the importance of proper planning and the Miracle of Life Insurance. By properly implementing strategies and products, our clients are able to provide protection for the ones they love and make sure that their financial goals will be fulfilled, even if they are no longer around. It is very gratifying for me to see Louise in such good financial shape after all these years. And it is heartwarming to know that those five grandchildren will always remember their trip to Disney World with Louise and Grampy John.

P. Shaun McDuffee, CLU, ChFC, AEP, CEPA
Senior Vice President, Senior Partner, North Star Resource Group

Many years ago, I conducted an educational seminar in Dallas. One of my interns did cold calls to invite people. One of the couples who agreed to attend my seminar, Heidi and Scott, were both pathologists. Scott did not want to go, but his wife told him, "I am going with or without you. I think our finances are kind of a mess, and we need some help." Scott was an absolutely brilliant individual. He developed a lot of the prostate cancer markers and tests that are used with patients today.

Scott was in his early forties, and Heidi was in her mid-thirties. They did not have any children, although he had a child from a previous marriage. Scott was not interested in talking to me at all. Heidi kind of dragged him to our meeting. But it turned out that he had a passion for wine, like I do, so we started talking about wine. One thing led to another, and we started working together. I put a financial plan in place for them based on their income. We did a variety of investments, and we picked up $5 million in life insurance for each of them, as well as about $17,000 a month in disability coverage. He really didn't want the coverage.

He said, "I don't see why I need life insurance. I don't see why I need disability insurance." We went back and forth. Finally, he said, "Look, if you are this convinced that I need this insurance, quite frankly I am going to do it just to get you off my back." His wife was definitely relieved, and we became really good friends. They did not live in Austin, as I do, but they would come to Austin once a year. My wife and I would go to dinner with them.

Six years ago, I got a text from Heidi on a Saturday morning at six o'clock. She said, "Scott and I have been up most of the night. We got some really bad news. Scott was diagnosed with rapidly progressing ALS [Lou Gehrig's disease.] Of all the things we are worrying about right now, I just thank God that we met you all those years ago because the one thing we don't have to worry about is our finances."

I met with them right away, and they said the doctors told Scott he had a maximum of five years to live. I would meet with them a couple of times a year and whenever he just needed to talk. Every time we met, interestingly enough, we never talked about their investments, although they had a couple million dollars' worth of investments with me. The only thing Scott wanted to talk about was to ask if I still had the life insurance in place. By this time, he was getting a $17,000-a-month payment from MetLife for disability. He was on claim with MetLife for almost

> He also got a lump-sum disability payment when he was first diagnosed, and that allowed him to buy a van and a special wheelchair.

four years. That claim enabled them to put an elevator in the house. He also got a lump-sum disability payment when he was first diagnosed, and that allowed him to buy a van and a special wheelchair. Eventually, that disability coverage covered in-home nursing for him. So they never had to tap into any of their financial resources; the disability coverage covered everything.

He passed away in April 2015. I knew he was pretty close to the end. I talked to Heidi at the end of the previous year, and she said he was beginning to lose respiratory control, which is the last stage. He hadn't been able to move anything but one finger for almost a year and a half.

When he passed, Heidi sent me an e-mail, and we talked. I said, "We are not going to make any financial decisions for four to six months. You have plenty of cash; you are in a good spot right now. Just take four to six months, and don't make any big financial decisions." She did that, and then she moved to another city to take a new job, kind of as a fresh start.

When I flew to see her recently, she and I laughed a little bit about how she had to drag Scott to that first meeting, and the last thing on the planet he wanted was life insurance.

The reality is, that is his legacy now. That life insurance is going to ensure that she is financially okay. Scott's child from his previous marriage received Scott's retirement account, so he will be okay as well.

Scott's disability insurance also included a death benefit, so Heidi got another $80,000 from that policy when he died. For a product that he didn't want anything to do with, it ended up paying $600,000 or $700,000.

Dan E. McGivern, CLU, RHU, CLTC
Financial Advisor, North Star Resource Group

I inherited a client, Jim, when I took over the Iowa City office. He contacted me to cancel his disability income policy. He said it was too expensive while he was completing his fellowship. I reviewed the coverage and made changes that cut his premiums in half but retained his future insurability options. With the savings, he purchased term life insurance to protect his wife, Katie, and their three small children.

Before he finished his training, I tried to contact Jim to make changes, but Katie would not pass on the message or let me in their home. She actually stopped me at the door.

When Jim finished training, they moved to the West Coast, and we continued to work over the phone and through the mail. He increased his disability income insurance and converted his life insurance but opted for a minimum premium until his practice got better.

Several years later, they called to tell me they were canceling the insurance because another agent had better coverage. I flew to Oregon to meet with them over a two-day period, and I preserved the business. Two years later, I received "the call" from Katie while I was attending the MDRT meeting in Chicago. Jim had been diagnosed with liver cancer, and the prognosis was not good. She was concerned about his disability income insurance and life insurance. I assured her that everything was in place to replace as much of his income as we could. They used some of the disability income benefit to keep the life insurance going until the waiver of premium rider started.

He was totally disabled for six years before his death. The waiver of premium rider kicked in after six months and started paying the "whole life" premium into his contract—an amount almost three times greater than what he had been paying. With the accumulated cash value, he was able to prepay and preplan his funeral and take that responsibility away from Katie. Jim's family was able to stay in their own home, and his children graduated from college without any student loans.

Katie and I still exchange Christmas cards each year to keep up with each other's families. She even wrote a letter to Bob Senkler, the former CEO of Securian Financial Group, to convey her story and show her gratitude.

> He was totally disabled for six years before his death. The waiver of premium rider kicked in after six months and started paying the "whole life" premium into his contract—an amount almost three times greater than what he had been paying.

Douglas Weisenberger, CFP®, CLTC
Senior Partner, North Star Resource Group

In April 1999, I was working with a lot of engineers, and one of my clients who was an engineer referred me to a thirty-six-year-old engineer we'll call Tim. His wife was thirty-four and was a stay-at-home mom. They had a son who was five years old, twin daughters who were three, and another son who was five months old at the time.

We got together to talk about their dreams, which are the same dreams we all have: good health, a happy retirement, watching your kids attend college, getting married, etc. They had only one income, so their money was tight, but we managed to get him to save a little bit of money. Term insurance was the best option for him because of the budget, for cash-flow reasons. We got everything set up.

Fast-forward two and a half years to August 2001. Tim called me and said he wanted to come see me. When I saw him in the lobby, I saw that his head was shaved. I jokingly said, "Nice summer 'do."

He said, "Well, that's what I want to talk to you about." He told me he had terminal cancer and had only a few months to live. He wanted to sit down with me and write a note to his wife about what she should be doing with the money and so forth.

It got a little emotional. Is that not the ultimate honor, when a dying man asks you to sit down and help him write a letter to his wife?

It turned out to be more of a list, and we named it the "what if" list. We spent the whole afternoon doing that, but it was all about helping a dying man find peace and remove one more worry. In August of that year, we got all of that done and said our good-byes. The next April, I was on a plane to a Securian convention. I opened up the local newspaper, and there was his obituary.

In June, his wife came to my office ready to start moving forward. I will never forget this. She had one piece of paper in her hand—the "what if" list. He had given it to her. She said, "You don't know how much this helped. Everybody came at me with, 'You should see my guy. You should do this. Do you have this covered?' I knew that you and my husband took care of it."

Due to this unique situation, we were able to convert his entire 401(k) and all taxable IRAs to Roth IRAs with no tax consequences. The house has been paid off for years. His wife's retirement is set. The oldest son is a junior in college, the twins are freshmen, and the youngest son just got his driver's license. Their mom has followed her dream—she got her teaching certificate and is now teaching. They didn't save enough money to pull this all off, but life insurance allowed it to happen.

> **They didn't save enough money to pull this all off, but life insurance allowed it to happen.**

It is all part of the whole financial planning process—you cover the basics first. Life insurance is least expensive way to cover that kind of risk, in my opinion.

I have been at North Star Resource Group for almost thirty-five years. I tell newer advisors, "If you are ever in that situation with a client, just ask them what things they are worrying about the most." Their family will be right at the top—the worry about their loved ones knowing what to do with money, and so forth.

I tell every client that life insurance is about leaving loved ones the ability to make choices and not be forced to make decisions.

୫୬

These stories are perfect examples of why North Star has kept the focus on protection for our clients. A financial plan is only as good as its foundation. If you don't have a good foundation, then things fall apart pretty quickly. That is why we always start by getting the foundation done right. Then we can build the wealth later. We build a lot of wealth, but we do it with a good foundation in place first—life insurance.

What a tragedy it is when someone passes away and has no coverage. We often see reports in the news of people who have died, and someone sets up a benefit in that person's name at a local bank. They ask people to contribute. Or someone will put a can on the cashier's counter at a restaurant, asking for donations for the family of someone who has passed away. When we see that, we know they didn't plan.

It is rare for people to die as young as these clients did, and it is rare for people to die soon after getting insurance in place. If a lot of people died right after securing protection, life insurance would be much more expensive. But that is why you do it—because you never know what will happen. And that is why life insurance is so inexpensive for young people in particular, because they are not supposed to die soon. Once purchased, a substantial life insurance policy could cost you just a couple hundred dollars a month in premium to retain.

Regardless of the cost, again, life insurance is a promise you keep to your family. That kind of peace of mind for the future is priceless.

THE VALUE OF LIFE INSURANCE: INSIGHT FROM THE INDUSTRY'S MOST RESPECTED LEADERS

CHAPTER 14

PAUL BLANCO, LUTCF

Founder and CEO

Barnum Financial Group

Shelton, Connecticut

Paul began his career in the financial services industry as a financial services representative with MetLife in 1991.

In just two years, Paul moved into management, taking over a small, seven-person MetLife office in Trumbull, Connecticut. As its CEO, Paul oversaw the expansion of Barnum Financial Group to the industry leading firm it is today. With thirty offices in Connecticut, New York, New Jersey, Massachusetts, and Rhode Island, Barnum Financial Group has clients in all fifty states and employs more than four hundred people.

In recognition of his efforts, Paul became the youngest inductee into the MetLife Managers' Hall of Fame in 2003. In 2006, he became the youngest winner of its Top of the Tower award, and in 2010, Paul became the youngest manager in MetLife's history to reach Golden Laureate status. He achieved Platinum Laureate status in 2015.

A consistent top performer, Paul has qualified for eight consecutive Management Leaders Conferences and fourteen America's Council Conferences. He received MetLife's prestigious Triskelion Award for outstanding management leadership in 2004, 2007, 2010, and 2014. Paul led the team at Barnum to be recognized as MetLife's Firm of the Year from 2004 through 2008 and in 2012 and 2013.

Paul has served on the GAMA Foundation's Board of Trustees and has qualified for GAMA's Master Agency Award and International Management Diamond Plus and Diamond Awards. GAMA has named his firm one of the top one hundred US financial agencies multiple times.

Paul has appeared on many radio and television programs, as well as in national and local publications, providing advice on leadership, philanthropy, recruiting, and financial services. A noted industry speaker, Paul has presented at numerous MetLife and industry events and at GAMA International's LAMP conference.

A prominent philanthropist in his community, Paul's ultimate dream is for 100 percent of his employees to give back to the community in some way. Barnum employees volunteer in support of programs like "Bikes for Kids" and "Backpacks for Kids" and building playgrounds through KaBOOM!

In 2007, the Fairfield County Remodelers and Home Building Association named Paul Philanthropist of the Year in 2007, and he was inducted into the Connecticut Business Hall of Fame and Junior Achievement Hall of Fame. The *Hartford Business Journal* named his firm as one of the "Best Places to Work in Connecticut" in 2006, 2009, 2010, and 2011, and the *Fairfield County Business Journal* awarded his firm the same honor in 2012. *Providence Business News* named Barnum Financial Group the "Best Place to Work in Rhode Island" from 2011 through 2014. Paul received the Greater Valley Chamber of Commerce Business Growth of the Year Award, the Westchester County Chabad Lubavitch Corporate Leadership Award, and the Valley United Way Community Impact Award.

Paul's passion for sports and youth in the community has inspired him to support a local football camp, a Little League team, an adult softball team, Junior Achievement, and the "Make a Difference Day" campaign.

In 2006, Paul and his wife, Mindee, started Foundation for Life, Inc., a 501(c)(3) organization established as a vehicle through which Barnum volunteers provide financial support to charities throughout their local communities. Since its inception, Foundation for Life has raised hundreds of thousands of dollars to support many local charities. (Foundation for Life is not affiliated with MetLife or any MetLife affiliate.)

PAUL'S STORY

The Advocacy and Creativity of Life Insurance Appealed to Me

When I was twenty-two years old, I was recruited into the industry. I loved the opportunity and saw this as an ideal career path. The company I started with was Metropolitan Life. I kid people and say we sold whole life and term insurance, basically.

> At a very young age, I was attracted to the advocacy piece of it and the creative ways you can solve problems using life insurance.

Not having any experience with life insurance, I was amazed at a couple of pieces of it. First, the power of what it did for people in case something bad happened kind of blew me away. I had no experience with it, and my parents did not even own it, as I found out. Second, I was amazed once I understood some of the benefits for people who own life insurance. So at a very young age, I was attracted to all those different pieces—the advocacy piece of it and the creative ways you can solve problems using life insurance. I saw myself as almost a teacher when I was out there.

Two Death Claims Early in My Career Showed me the Power of Life Insurance

I had two experiences with death claims within my first four months in the business, in 1991. They made a huge impact on me.

The first death claim happened after I had been in the business for only two months, in 1991. One day, a lady named Teresa walked into our office in Brooklyn and said she needed to do a death claim for her sister. It was about $25,000, which was a huge amount to her. I met Teresa in the lobby, and I was terrified because I had never done that before. I ran back to the office manager and said, "What are the forms? What do I do? How do I do this?" She walked me through it.

So I met Teresa in one of our conference rooms and helped her through the whole process. I guess I handled it in a warm, loving, professional manner because when I was done, she said to me, "I can't thank you enough for the way you handled this." She told me about the impact this check would have on her family. Then she said, "I know you don't make any money on this, and you did such a great job, so I want to buy something from you. I want to buy life insurance for my nephew." I sold her a $25,000 policy for her nephew.

My second death claim happened as the result of a visit I made to the company my wife, Mindee, worked for. She was the VP of Operations for a furniture company at the time. So I went in and wrote health insurance for the company. I asked the owner if I could offer life insurance to the employees, and he said, "You're welcome to talk to everybody." So I wrote a bunch of life insurance. One of the employees I wrote was a young man named Juan who had moved to the northeastern United States from Puerto Rico. His job was basically to move the furniture around. He was a baseball player like me. He was a big, strong kid, about 6'1". He used to pick up sofa beds to move them. I wrote him a $15,000 life insurance policy based on what he could afford and what he needed.

About three months later, Juan's parents called Mindee and told her that as Juan was on his way home the previous Friday night, he had a brain aneurysm and died in an alley. On Monday morning, the parents showed up at my office from Puerto Rico, speaking Spanish. I didn't understand them, but I understood the love and the hugs and the kisses they gave me. The funeral home called my office. Until we gave them a certified letter, they wouldn't give Juan a burial.

Leaders Serve Two Main Clients

Growing up, I was always captain of my athletic teams—football, baseball, and track. I wanted to be in leadership in this industry, too. When I walked into my first interview, the manager asked me where I saw myself in five years. I asked him how long it took him to get the role he had. He seemed extremely successful, and I knew he was leading people. I said I wanted to do the same thing. So very early on, I knew I wanted to be in a corporate leadership position, not knowing what it was, really. Once I finished my first year as a producer, I became an associate branch manager. I started teaching and developing people around me. Then I got a chance to move to Connecticut and take over what is now Barnum Financial Group, but at that time, it was a bankrupt place that had only seven advisors. I took my message of protecting and caring about people to the firm.

I looked at it as having two clients. One was my group of advisors—I needed to develop them. The second was the people who were buying products from the advisors. And that started my journey. About five years in, during the late 1990s, 100 percent of our revenue came from life insurance. Then in the late 1990s, we started asset gathering. But about 40 percent of our business is still protection sales. It's at the top of the pyramid when you talk about financial planning. You have to have your life insurance in place, or else it's a failed plan.

Advice for Consumers: Life Insurance Is the Foundation of Your Financial Success

Consumers have to look at life insurance as the building block to their financial success. It's one of the first things you have to purchase. We offer a "starter kit," and it contains everything a young family needs: life insurance, disability, and a Roth IRA. That's really the foundation of any good financial plan.

It Is Our Responsibility as Leaders to Make Risk Protection a Priority

> I spend every waking moment encouraging my leadership team to understand that it is our responsibility to ensure that our clients are protected.

Our industry is taking the road of least resistance. I spend every waking moment encouraging my leadership team to understand that it is our responsibility to ensure that our clients are protected. I recently received an e-mail that Phil Richards of North Star Resource Group sent to me. It is a note that Shaun McDuffee e-mailed to his team in Austin last year, and I have used it a ton. He ended the note by saying, "I'm not going to let this happen on my watch." And that, philosophically, is how we lead this organization.

Here is the e-mail Shaun wrote to his team:

From: McDuffee, Shaun

Sent: Saturday, June 6, 2015, 6:08 PM

To: NS McDuffee Office <NSMcDuffeeOffice@northstarfinancial.com>

Subject: Interesting stat

Hi Gang —

After June, I will be sending a more detailed report from the overall dinner tracker, but I was looking at this while on the airplane from Hawaii. A very telling stat jumped out at me that I would like each of you to think about because I think it's crucial that we remedy this.

We have had more than 10k units attend dinner the past six years (Yeah!). We have approximately 2,000 clients (20%—would prefer 25%), but the stat that jumped out at me was that we as a division have only protected *half* of our clients' families (or future families) with life insurance. This is mind-blowing.

Almost 1,000 families or clients were brought aboard and *not* given life insurance. Given that there is almost no situation where someone could qualify for disability insurance and *not* qualify for life (I actually can't think of one single case where that would be the situation), I am actually blown away by this.

When we all came into this business, one of the key things we stated was that we wanted to make a difference in the lives of our clients.

How can we say we are making a difference if we are not intervening and convincing our clients to spend $50 to $100 per month to protect their families and/or future insurability??????

I really want each of us to focus on helping out clients understand that they must do this. It's imperative, and it's almost malpractice not to help them do this. Do you want to be the person who has to face a client who loses their insurability and be the one to tell them, **"Yeah, my bad. I should be been more convincing. Oops…"?** Anyone who pushes back needs to see how convicted you are.

I just delivered a $5.3M death claim on someone who told me they didn't *need* life insurance—now his spouse has nearly unlimited options. This was on top of a $17k/month DI policy they said they didn't want or need as well. That DI claim paid out over $750,000 of income replacement for $40,000 of premium. The client pushed back on me three times, and I refused to budge. I wouldn't have been able to look myself in the mirror if he had died or when he went on a DI claim if I hadn't done that. This stuff happens, and it's why I love what I do for a living. The investments are great, the fee plans are nifty…**the insurance is where I changed that family forever.**

Recently I have jokingly made a few comments to some people who were submitting DI without life apps. I am going to be more forceful on this, as this is awful. One out of two clients we bring in we are not being protected, and that can't and won't happen on my watch, my friends. This career is about getting people to do what they *need* to do…not what is easy and what they *want* to do.

Sorry for the ranting, but this statistic is really awful, and I know that every person in this division is better than this. **Changing lives, forever starts with this key piece.** Everyone, please take a moment, rethink the language in Insurance 101s, and let's make this our *mission*. Moving forward, **NO ONE BECOMES A CLIENT WITHOUT BUYING LIFE INSURANCE (if they are insurable).** I love you guys, and as your leader, I have to call this out. Let's make sure that with every review we do with existing clients, we review their life insurance and make sure we cover their human life value.

Thanks, my friends!

PS: It's a *great* day to be a financial advisor and part of the Lone Star/North Star family!

Shaun

What Shaun was doing there was taking responsibility for taking his eye off the most important thing we can do for clients.

Advice to Agents and Advisors: Investments May Be Cooler, But It's Our Responsibility to Protect Our Clients' Futures with Life Insurance

There are really only two ways you can grow a business. It's very simple: you can see more people or sell bigger cases. Well, the reason financial planning became prevalent is because it's very hard to wake up and say, "I'm going to look for just affluent people." So if you're seeing people and you're selling multiple products in the households, your business and your case size get way bigger. You don't have to sit with more people; you can drive the size of your cases.

We teach advisors to slow it down, build a wall around your clients, and make sure you're looking at the client's complete financial situation. Educate yourself, and use that education to find out exactly what the client needs. If you pull into a place where your car gets serviced and say, "It's not running well," the guy isn't going to say, "Yeah, you need a tune-up." He needs to look at the car first. How can you give good financial advice if you're not looking at every part of their financial house?

> **How can you give good financial advice if you're not looking at every part of their financial house?**

Also, it's okay if you don't enjoy selling life insurance, but you need to understand the miracle and the advocacy of what it means. Partner with someone. Put a protection person on your team. At Barnum, we have three life insurance wholesalers who work for my firm. They are on my payroll, and they are segmented in terms of small, medium, and large cases. We are helping our advisors have enough knowledge to be dangerous, but if you don't want to do it, we will come in and do it for you. We have had extremely positive results with this approach. The first advisor we started with is a star; he has been doing it for six years now. Last year, we did a little over $26 million, a phenomenal amount of target premium.

It is our responsibility to ensure that our clients are protected with life insurance. To make this point when I meet with recruits, I always use an illustration on a piece of paper. I draw a circle on the right side of the page, and I write above it "investments and income." In that circle, I list mutual funds, stocks, bonds, annuities, options, 529s, and DPPs [direct purchase plans]. I ask, "Who sells all those?" The recruit will name all types of companies and wirehouses. Then on the left side of the page, I draw another circle and label it "protection." Inside that circle, I write "life insurance, disability, health insurance, auto, and home." And I ask, "Who sells that?"

The recruit will say, "Insurance companies."

Then I'll ask, "Which one would you rather sell?" We're recruiting a lot of Millennials off college campuses. They all choose the investment income. When I ask why, they'll say, "It's cooler. And I can make more money."

I'll reply, "Okay, that might be true. But let me show you something." I draw one more circle at the bottom of the page, so now there are two at the top and one at the bottom, and I connect them. The third one is called "financial planning." I show them that 50 percent of our business comes from planning and protection, and 50 percent comes from assets. And I say, "Listen, if your client has a portfolio that earns 6 or 8 percent, whatever that number is, but he doesn't have the proper life insurance and he dies prematurely, his family is in trouble. If he doesn't have the proper disability insurance and he becomes disabled and can't make an income, his family is in trouble. If he doesn't have the right umbrella policy and his dog bites someone, the family is in trouble."

> I try to help them understand that yes, investments might be cooler, and you might make more, but protecting clients is your responsibility.

So I try to help them understand that yes, investments might be cooler, and you might make more, but protecting clients is your responsibility.

Let's Leverage Technology to Make the Process Easier

I think the industry has changed dramatically from when we started; the margins on our products and the renewal part of our products have changed. I think that leaders who didn't grow up on this side of the business have taken shortcuts. It's a lot harder to ask for money than to just move money, so people avoid selling risk-protection products. I think all those things came into play, and then the complexity of the products has changed. All of this has made it very difficult for advisors and companies to stay focused on the things that matter.

Revenue is revenue, but you have to make sure the consumer's entire financial situation is taken care of. As a leader, it's not popular to challenge a producer who's doing $1 million of GDC about his life insurance goal. But that's my responsibility. So I think the industry has fallen away from it, and I think underwriting has gotten a little more difficult.

Today we do a lot of business over the phone using DocuSign, and you don't even have to meet with clients; they can sign online. I think the next thing the industry is going to have to do is reduce the wait time to get underwriting approved. When you go shopping in a department store, you have to wait in line at the register. But when you go to the Apple store, they come up to you and scan your purchase into their phone, and your purchase is done. I think the industry is going to have to fix how the process affects the consumer. It's not as bad as the mortgage industry, but it's still bad. If we can improve the way people make purchases, it will help the advisors too. Look at the EKGs that doctors used in the 1990s, and compare them to the Fitbit devices we now use to monitor our vital signs. The technology is out there. How can we make our process simpler?

> If we can improve the way people make purchases, it will help the advisors too.

Those Who "Get It" Will Continue to Evolve

I think this is the greatest time ever to be in this industry. I think we're going to see continuous consolidation, but we're also going to see fewer qualified advisors, which unfortunately will affect the consumer. But the people who get it will have an incredible opportunity to impact people's lives at all levels. There is no other way to distribute these products. The robo-advisors will take a segment of the market, and consumers can get some education about financial products online. But to help people do real planning with life insurance, disability insurance, estate planning, and all assets at the forefront, it's complex and needs to be done face to face. The people who understand that will continue to evolve.

> To help people do real planning with life insurance, disability insurance, estate planning, and all assets at the forefront, it's complex and needs to be done face to face.

The other piece of that is you're going to have to get a little uncomfortable. That's what people are forgetting—that you're going to go through obstacles, like the Department of Labor and robo-advisors, and you're going to have to step out of your comfort zone a little bit to challenge your own thinking and look at distribution differently. The advisors who do that are going to blow away the industry.

We also need to look at different ways to distribute training and development. Things are going to change rapidly. We need more industry leaders who give back to The American College and GAMA. We need more leaders to understand that it's their responsibility to support the greatest industry that we've all been very blessed to be a part of. We have to do our best to continue to make it grow.

Life insurance is one of the most powerful products I've ever seen, and it can be used in many, many different ways. I feel that my responsibility to my advisors, the industry, and the general public is to spread that message as fast and as effectively as possible for me to do my part to impact the problem we have with people not having enough protection. So I'm going to keep doing that and keep trying to influence others.

⏳ CHAPTER 15
TOM BURNS,
CLU, CHFC

Chief Distribution Officer

Allianz Life Insurance Company of North America

Minneapolis, Minnesota

Tom Burns leads the overall direction of sales and distribution across all business lines for Allianz Life Insurance Company of North America (Allianz Life®). In this role, he is responsible for developing and maximizing distribution through strategic relationships in the independent, wirehouse, and bank channels, as well as through owned and independent insurance field marketing offices and Allianz Life's retail broker/dealer, Questar Capital Corporation.

Before joining Allianz Life in 2006, Tom served as senior vice president of Securian Advisory Services. Before joining Securian, he was vice president of third-party marketing at Prudential Select, a subsidiary of Prudential Financial, Inc.

Tom has a bachelor of science degree in economics from South Dakota State University. He is active in the Association for Advanced Life Underwriting and is a past president of the LIMRA Distribution Leaders Round Table.

TOM'S STORY

A Believer in Life Insurance at Age Twenty-One

My love affair with life insurance began when I was twenty-one years old. My father had been a life insurance agent with Prudential for thirty years in our small town of Luverne, Minnesota, and I had just joined his practice right off the college campus.

I'll never forget it—I was in the middle of my new-hire training with Prudential when my dad became ill. At the time, we thought it was just the flu, but suddenly he passed away with an aneurysm at the young age of fifty-seven. I was the one who found him, and that was something I will never forget. Just like that, my dad was gone from our lives.

> My mom was able to remain in her home and maintain her lifestyle because of the life insurance my dad had provided for her.

I found out very quickly what life insurance meant to my mother and our family. My mom was able to remain in her home and maintain her lifestyle because of the life insurance my dad had provided for her—because of the planning that my father had done for his family. Right away, at age twenty-one, I was a believer in the value of life insurance, and it was a lesson that has defined much of my personal and professional life.

A Career That Helps People and Provides a Flexible Schedule

Watching my father while I was growing up made me want to follow his footsteps and become a life insurance agent and financial professional. We lived in a small community, and he was Mr. Insurance Guy. He was well-respected, and some of his best clients were also his best friends. So I thought, "What a neat industry—you get to make your living by helping people, and you get to work every day with people you like."

I also saw that his career allowed him to have a flexible schedule. He never missed one of my baseball games, whether we were in Minnesota, South Dakota, New Mexico, or Texas. I played four years of college baseball, and he was at every game. He was my best friend.

I realized later why he was able to attend all of my baseball games. Having his own business—running his own practice as a financial professional—allowed him to be there for each of the events and activities that were important to me and the other members of our family.

I definitely wanted to have a family, and I wanted to be part of whatever activities they were going to be involved in. I knew that becoming a financial professional like my dad would enable me to be there for my kids and family—just like he was for us growing up.

Advice to Agents and Financial Professionals: Have the Courageous Conversations

It is critical for financial professionals to start with a foundation of life insurance as they are building their clients' financial plans for the future. Make sure the basics—the life insurance needs—are taken care of first, before you get into all the financial planning and investments. Somebody who cares about his or her family will be willing to take the necessary steps to make sure that if there is a premature death or disability, the family's needs and lifestyle are protected. As I saw with my own parents, life insurance does not fill a hypothetical need. It protects real families with real needs that can be filled only by the benefits that life insurance provides.

> As I saw with my own parents, life insurance does not fill a hypothetical need. It protects real families with real needs that can be filled only by the benefits that life insurance provides.

Life insurance doesn't have the pizzazz that investments have, but it is absolutely necessary. So have that courageous conversation with your consumers about the Miracle of Life Insurance—about what it can do for a family—and the fact that it's not just a death benefit.

Early on, I purchased cash-value life insurance. Throughout my career, I became involved with a few businesses, and it was very helpful to have access to the available cash value from those policies, to be able to take loans from the cash value and then pay them back. There is a lot of flexibility with cash-value life insurance. So my advice for a financial professional is this: do not prepare a financial strategy for any client without first ensuring that the foundation is solid with life insurance.

Advice to Clients: Find a Financial Professional, and Buy Life Insurance While You're Young

My three kids are Millennials, and they are all grown up and off the payroll. I tell them what I would tell any consumer: find a financial professional. Don't do it by yourself. And I advise people to get a financial professional who is *balanced*. What I mean by that is that they need to have the courageous conversation with a financial professional to find out about life insurance *now*, while they are young, and how much life insurance they truly need. Build that foundation first. The investments and all the other financial products can help you grow assets. But looking at my family and my three kids—they are consumers. I want to make sure that they find a trusted financial professional out there who will give them the knowledge and information they need.

Consumers have to have life insurance. I don't care if it's term insurance or cash value, but get it early. You don't ever think you are going to die young or become uninsurable, but it happens.

Why not buy life insurance while you are young, insurable, and healthy?

Let's Recruit, Train, and Develop More Financial Professionals to Serve Future Clients

My major concern for the future of our industry is that there are fewer firms like North Star that are bringing in and training new financial professionals into our industry. Everyone has heard the statistics—the average age of a financial professional is fifty-seven to fifty-eight years old. How are we going to fix that? We have a couple of programs here at Allianz to bring new financial professionals into the business, but I think more and more insurance companies are going to have to change their focus and start recruiting the next generation of financial professionals.

> I think more and more insurance companies are going to have to change their focus and start recruiting the next generation of financial professionals.

As an industry, we also need to increase our focus on training and developing these newer financial professionals. I am a big fan of team structures in financial professional practices, where you bring new financial professionals into an established practice and they learn the business by watching and emulating successful financial professionals. We are doing a fair amount of that at Questar Capital, our retail broker/dealer. We are bringing in newer financial professionals and pairing them with experienced financial professionals within a team, very similar to what happens at larger firms like UBS and Merrill Lynch. I would like to see much more of this type of model across the industry because otherwise, we are going to run into a situation where we are going to not have enough financial professionals to take care of the needs of future consumers.

I also don't think there is enough training and focus on that courageous sale of life insurance. It is easier to train financial professionals to gather assets—no question about it. Gathering assets under management is an easier conversation than having that important yet courageous conversation about life insurance as the basic foundation of your financial-strategy recommendations.

We need to get back to the basics to best prepare our industry for the needs of future generations of consumers.

CHAPTER 16

J. SCOTT DAVISON,

CLU, CHFC

President and CEO

OneAmerica

Indianapolis, Indiana

Scott serves as president and CEO of the companies of OneAmerica®. He leads OneAmerica's nationwide network of companies and affiliates. The OneAmerica companies offer a wide variety of products, including retirement plan products and services, individual life insurance, annuities, asset-based long-term care solutions, and employee benefits.

Scott was appointed president in 2013 and CEO in 2014. His almost thirty-year career in the insurance industry began at UNUM, where he served in a variety of financial roles, including CFO of UNUM's Duncanson & Holt reinsurance subsidiary. In 2000, Scott joined OneAmerica as vice president and later senior vice president of strategic planning and corporate development. In 2004, he was appointed chief financial officer, a post he held until his promotion to executive vice president in 2011. The *Indianapolis Business Journal* named him CFO of the Year in 2008.

Scott serves on the boards of LIMRA/LOMA LL Global and the Million Dollar Round Table Foundation and is a trustee of The American College. He's also a board member of Indiana University Health, the Indiana Chamber of Commerce, Central Indiana Corporate Partnership, and Indiana Sports Corporation.

He holds a bachelor of arts degree in economics and history from Middlebury College in Vermont and a Master of Business Administration from the University of Southern Maine. He is an alumnus of Harvard Business School's advanced management program.

SCOTT'S STORY

My Introduction to Life Insurance

My understanding of the importance of life insurance developed gradually, starting with my first job out of college.

I took it because the company was in a place I wanted to live, and I liked the idea that it provided service to people. This was important to me. I come from a family in which everyone is a pastor or social worker or does other service. My sister and I are the only ones in business.

Over time, especially after reading more than a thousand claims files as an auditor, I realized insurance is an even greater force for good than I'd initially imagined.

When My Passion for Life Insurance Turned Personal

A few years ago, something happened that elevated my appreciation for our industry to a new level. It's a story I tell every new home-office associate in our company and often repeat to our field partners.

Our neighbors were a great couple with two young children. We became friends, and our youngest kids still spend a lot of time together. About eight or nine years into the friendship, we learned that the forty-nine-year-old dad had a brain tumor known as a glioblastoma.

In the eighteen months between his diagnosis and death, even though he was a good friend and had a great job as an attorney for a major international company, he got uncomfortable when I tried to bring up life insurance. I accepted that he didn't want to mix business and friendship.

Toward the end, when he was in the hospital, his wife called me in tears one evening. She said she was writing checks and didn't know if there was money to cover them. She was starting to panic, afraid she should sell the house and look for a job, even though she'd been out of the workforce since her first child was born.

"I have all this paperwork from all these financial institutions," she said. "Can you look at it and tell me where I am? I just need to know the truth."

When I arrived in their kitchen, she was calmer but still crying. I was worried, thinking, "If he didn't tell you in the last eighteen months that you are all good, then it's probably not all good."

I started going through a big stack of papers, the same kind of material we send to people. I saw that her husband had been a saver; there was a nice balance in his 401(k) plan. I found stock options from his employer, as well as a brokerage account. The numbers were good, but not great.

Then, about two-thirds into the pile, I started finding the life insurance. Her husband's company had an enormous group term buy-up with us, and it was an unusually large number. He also had some whole life insurance with another mutual company any of us would be proud to represent.

I broke into a cold sweat when I saw this stuff. I turned to her and said, "Here's the deal. There's a lot to work on, but you don't have to do anything right now. You have enough to pay the bills, and you can keep writing checks. Don't change anything in your life. Take care of your husband; take care of your kids. You and I will work through this later. But you don't have to sell the house, and if you choose, you can meet the school bus every day for as long as the kids are in school. Also, they'll  be able to go to college wherever they can get in. You'll have to be really smart about this, but there is enough."

Her relief was palpable. She was in tears again, but it was a different kind of crying.

That was in October 2009. My friend died on December 2. It was a great relief, knowing that in the time before and after his death, his wife could focus on her loved ones.

Today, she and the kids live in the same house, and our families are still friends. She and her children have taken amazing vacations to Europe and the western United States. These trips have brought them closer and have helped—as much as anything could—fill the void my friend's death left. The daughter is applying to colleges and will probably get into a good one. Because of life insurance, she can afford her choice, even if it costs more than $60,000 a year.

My friend's decision to take care of his family was an act of love in its purest form.

Several things saved this family from financial crisis. One is the Miracle of Life Insurance. Another is the team who provided it. The people who set up the group plan got the 5X buy-up for my friend. Additional people, including the individual career agent from the other mutual company, encouraged him to do the right thing for his family.

When I share this story with new OneAmerica associates, a few people are crying by the time I'm done. Sometimes I'm crying. And I'm always grateful for the reminder that we work in an industry that helps American families every day.

Advice to Clients: An Integrated Approach Is Best

There's another story I like to tell, one that shows how insurance is a pivotal part of a solid financial plan. At OneAmerica, we believe an integrated approach is the most appropriate for client well-being. While it's great to have market-facing assets, and we are a big player in the 401(k) business. People need some fixed money that is safe and guaranteed.

With cash-value life insurance or fixed annuities in their portfolios, people who happen to retire at a time of market turmoil—such as we experienced in August 2008—can weather the financial storm.

Without intending to, my parents implemented this strategy. My dad still has the life insurance policy he bought in 1949. When they retired, my parents annuitized half their assets because a caring agent told them that's what they should do. They are smart, educated people, but they don't know much about money. They followed the advice, and now they have a little bit in the market, a life insurance buffer, and paychecks for life. During the financial crisis, they didn't have to change their retirement plan one bit.

The system we promote with agents teaches a similar approach—of starting with a foundation of life insurance. Agents who learn to guide people in that direction will be powerful advocates and partners who will never lack clients.

Advice to Agents and Advisors: Stick with Life Insurance

I tell agents to stick with what's true. Permanent life insurance has always been a powerful financial tool that works in any market environment.

Some in our industry have been distracted into focusing primarily on transactional business, such as mutual funds or variable annuities. While this part of the business certainly has its place, these advisors risk having their practices damaged by regulators or trial attorneys. In my opinion, it's better to work at showing clients why it's smart to include life insurance as part of an integrated financial plan.

In the current regulatory climate, putting people in a life insurance policy alongside a well-considered plan is a defendable position. You can look anyone in the eye and say, "I did the right thing for this person. And I will do it again every time."

Let's Teach People about Sound Financial Planning

I've long pondered why our industry has moved from focusing on this life-changing product. I've decided there are two reasons:

1. People are overloaded with information. What sells is what's easy to describe. Permanent life insurance takes some time to explain.

2. People are seduced by examples of stock-market success. But for each person who strikes it rich, there are many who fail to achieve a sound financial footing in retirement.

It's up to our industry to educate people about the importance of a base of fixed money and a plan that includes elements that can't be whipsawed by inevitable market fluctuations.

We face several challenges. One is that this approach to financial planning doesn't easily lend itself to a fifteen-second sound bite. Another is that the mutual-fund industry has grown faster than our industry, as many advisors have drifted toward selling mutual funds rather than focus on life insurance.

However, I believe the best way to build an enduring practice and improve our industry's relevance is to do what a robo-advisor can't: build comprehensive financial plans that reflect each client's unique circumstances and appropriately blend market-facing assets with protection products and money sources that are safe and guaranteed.

This approach is the best policy for advisors and their clients.

⌛ CHAPTER 17

CAROLINE FEENEY,

CLU, CHFC

President, Prudential Advisors

The Prudential Insurance Company of America

Greater New York City Area

Caroline began her career with Prudential in 1993 as a financial professional. She soon moved into field management, where she held a number of positions and was consistently recognized as one of the company's leaders. She moved to the home office in 1998 and held a variety of senior leadership positions, including Vice President of Recruiting and Development and Eastern Territory Vice President, a position in which she was responsible for fourteen firms across nine states. In 2012, Caroline was named President of Prudential Advisors, the company's national sales organization.

Caroline has been featured as a main-platform speaker for industry events, such as GAMA International's annual LAMP meeting. She serves on The American College Board of Trustees and is a member of the board's Executive Committee. In 2016, Caroline was elected to serve a three-year term on the LIMRA Distribution Leaders Roundtable Executive Planning Committee.

In 2013, the National Council for Research on Women honored Caroline with its Trailblazer Award. The same year, *Working Mother* magazine recognized her as Prudential's Working Mother of the Year. In 2014, Executive Women of New Jersey honored her as Prudential's Policy Maker.

Caroline graduated from Bucknell University and has an MBA from Columbia University.

CAROLINE'S STORY

A Little Experience Makes All the Difference

After I graduated from Bucknell, for about a year and a half, I went down the expected professional path of starting a management training program—in the banking industry. Truthfully, I was bored. It wasn't fulfilling. I found it increasingly hard to get out of bed in the morning. Looking back, I understand it better—I got the paycheck but didn't get the purpose.

When I moved to Prudential in my early twenties, I accepted a position as a recruiter, to bring in financial professionals to a firm in New Jersey. The Managing Director wanted me to get some sales experience, and to my surprise, I really enjoyed it. Soon, however, I was asked to move into a role as manager of recruiting in the firm, which was great but would have meant giving up on selling.

My Managing Director allowed me to continue selling and working with clients while taking on the new recruiting responsibilities.

I then started doing joint work with the new financial professionals I helped bring on, and I really loved coaching them. Before I knew it, the sales skills I developed, the recruiting experience, and the coaching work I had done led to a sales manager role.

I remember making a pledge to myself, a wish, that I would love what I did and never be bored again. Although I didn't think I would wind up in the role I'm in now, I got my wish because I have never been bored a day since—in any of my roles. Maybe I wished too hard.

A Turning Point for Life Insurance

Thinking back, I can't say that when I came into this industry I had a love affair with life insurance. I liked the idea of insurance, understood it, and could explain it to people, but that was it—no true passion. However, as my career progressed, the value of life insurance became clearer. I recall three widows in particular—all lost their husbands under very different circumstances. Two of the men who died were in their forties. One had Crohn's disease, and the other one had a massive heart attack shoveling snow one especially tough winter. Seeing firsthand the impact the death benefit was able to make—that Prudential was able to make—was a very memorable feeling. It's hard to describe, but when you see life insurance in action, understand the circumstances around it, and know how it's going to help, I think you can truly understand the power it brings.

That's when I really developed the passion for what we're doing. Part of it, I think, is the multiplier effect—in this business, we are touching and impacting so many lives. That brings meaning, and I feel good about that. It motivates me.

A Management Role Began to Make Perfect Sense

Even at a relatively young age, I was able to see the impact I was having by bringing people into this business. I was able to work with people twice my age, or older, and help them develop plans to make more of an impact and to make their businesses grow. That was energizing to me. And all of a sudden, a role in leadership made sense to me. I'm a big believer that you need a real reason to jump out of bed in the morning and have some sort of purpose or mission.

Advice to Agents and Advisors: See the World from Clients' Point of View

The first thing is, try to understand the world from your clients' point of view. Understand that their situation is not only monetary—really get to know them. Take the time to learn about their families, their backgrounds, what their purposes are. Focus and work from the very first introduction to establish a deep and lasting relationship. I believe this forms the basis for success.

> Your job, first and foremost, is to help your client try to comprehend and understand their situation and help them make their dreams a reality.

The other thing I always say to financial advisors is to understand that your job really isn't about selling a client anything. Your job, first and foremost, is to help your client try to comprehend and understand their situation and help them make their dreams a reality. Where do they want to be, and where do they see themselves, five, ten, and twenty years from now? Help them find a way to get there. That may come in the form of a product sale or simply financial advice and guidance.

I strongly believe that when financial advisors understand their purpose and why they are in the business, the success and money will follow. It always does. So my advice is not to worry about it—worry about doing the right thing for your clients.

I think the group coming into the business today, the Millennials, really understands this fact and are poised to be successful. They are less about "Tell me how much money I can make." They are so much more about "Tell me the difference I can make in people's lives." I'm feeling very optimistic about our industry because of this.

It also helps to really think through the reality of what happens in people's lives when everything changes and how what you do can make a difference. In fact, on a personal note, my very dearest friend, who is only three years older than me and is like a sister to me, was just diagnosed with ovarian cancer. These types of life-changing events can happen to anyone, and while we can't stop them from happening or see them coming, we can be prepared. You can help your clients be prepared. They likely don't want to think about it, which is why your role is even more important.

Ask Yourself This One Critical Question Regarding Every Client

We need to accept the overall responsibility for coming up with holistic financial solutions and taking care of clients' needs. I think people should challenge themselves. When financial advisors say they are taking care of their clients' best interests, but the only thing they are caring for is managed money, I really think they should challenge themselves and ask themselves this question: "If something happens to my client in the next twelve months, have I really done all that I should for them?" People don't think about it that way when they are in their thirties or forties, when the worst is not supposed to happen. But it can, and it does.

If someone has been at this for twenty years as an asset manager and that is how he sees himself, and he doesn't even know where to begin to make life insurance part of his practice, the best thing he can do is just team up with somebody who makes life insurance part of their practice. We don't do enough of that as an industry. We do some joint work, but it would really benefit everyone if more financial advisors came up with a bona fide plan to surround themselves with a specialist who focuses on writing life insurance. They can help their clients that way. You do not have to always go it alone—reach out to those around you.

Advice to Consumers: Focus on the Future, and Find an Advisor to Guide You

Many people think about what they want to buy today. But it is important to think about tomorrow and the holistic picture of the future. Consumers always need to remember what is important in their lives. It goes both ways—understand what's important to you, and also have a financial advisor who understands what is important to you and why. Is it family, friends? Spending more time out of the office? Is it saving money for children or grandchildren to go to college? Or buying a pool for the backyard so your whole family can get together for some great family time? Is it paying down debt so you can sleep at night? People need to be able to articulate to an advisor what's important to them. And the advisor is in a position to help them overcome financial obstacles and reach their goals.

Select an advisor who is committed to his or her professional development and education and who represents a strong, solid, respectable firm.

Do your homework before you hire somebody, just like you would do your homework if you needed a medical specialist.

We Need to Make Life Insurance Sales Less Daunting

Let's face it—the whole life insurance process and the way life insurance is written today can be a daunting process. A lot of people are looking at different types of predictive analytics to get away from some of the underwriting details, but we're not there yet. It's a complicated, time-consuming, intrusive process. For that reason, I think both advisors and consumers may tend to focus more on asset management than on risk management—clients don't want to focus on having that discussion, and advisors don't drive that discussion enough. That creates a situation that could leave people unprotected. Financial advisors, instead of always navigating to where the client wants to go, should make sure they are looking at the holistic picture and bringing up solutions that may be tougher to discuss.

Technology Gives Us a Beneficial "High-Touch, High-Tech" Approach

Because technology has changed so much and will continue to change so rapidly, I believe it is going to change some of the complexity and some of the arduous nature of the life insurance approval process in general. I think we're going to have more and more companies leveraging all the medical data that are available—data analytics, predictive underwriting—so that our process is not quite so intrusive.

I am hopeful about the future of the industry. I believe there is a very, very strong place for advisors to differentiate themselves from so much that's out there today in terms of direct online sales and robo-advisors, through true advice. I don't think you can replace the value of an advisor understanding clients' needs, balanced against their background, short- and long-term goals, and dreams. We will always need to have relationships with our clients because of that dynamic, its complexity, and because clients want a little bit more hand holding sometimes. They will need an advisor to guide them through life's challenges, make sure their families are protected, and ensure that all of their needs are covered.

I am a big believer in what I call "high-touch, high-tech." I don't believe our advisors should feel threatened about being replaced by technology. Instead, we should view technology as an enabler, as a way to reach more people in a more efficient manner. It will put advisors in front of so many more clients than they could have seen otherwise. Technology enables us to connect with people we may not have normally come to know and stay in touch with them over time. And that lays the groundwork for sustainability and helps ensure long-term success.

CHAPTER 18

MARVIN H. FELDMAN,

CLU, CHFC, RFC

President, Feldman Financial Group

Clearwater, Florida

President and CEO, Life Happens

Washington, DC

Marv started his career as an agent with New York Life in Columbus, Ohio, in 1967, immediately after graduating from Ohio State University. After two and a half years in the field, he transitioned into New York Life's management program. In 1974, he returned to personal production in East Liverpool, Ohio, as a partner in the Feldman Agency and president of Fremar Financial Group.

He has been a member of the Million Dollar Round Table for forty-two years and served as MDRT president in 2002. He has been a member of the elite Top of the Table for thirty-four years, serving on the board and as the Top of the Table chairman. In 2004, the Million Dollar Round Table Foundation honored Marv as its Circle of Life recipient in recognition of his community and industry leadership.

Marv is a member of the National Association of Insurance and Financial Advisors, the Society of Financial Service Professionals, the International Association of Registered Financial Consultants, Forum 400, and the Association for Advanced Life Underwriting. He is a past secretary of the New York Life Agent's Advisory Council.

In 2011, Marv was named to Insurance Newscast's list of the one hundred most powerful people in the insurance industry in North America. In 2011, he was presented with the John Newton Russell Award, the highest honor the insurance industry bestows on an individual. He is listed in *Who's Who in Business and Finance* and *Who's Who in the World*. He contributes articles to many professional journals and has been featured in magazines and books. He has made speeches in thirty-six countries.

MARV'S STORY

Growing Up in the Life Insurance Business

I just turned seventy years old, and I have been in the business seventy years—I was born into the business. My dad used to practice his presentations on my brother and me when we were sitting at the kitchen table or wherever we happened to be. His philosophy was that if he could make it simple enough for my brother and me to understand, then it should be okay for a prospect or a client to understand.

> My dad used to practice his presentations on my brother and me when we were sitting at the kitchen table or wherever we happened to be.

All the years I was growing up, he was practicing his presentations. Every time we went out as a family, my mother always had a little notepad and a pencil with her. He was thinking of power phrases, thoughts, and ideas, and she was always scribing those down so that he could review them, think about them, and refine them as time went on.

So I grew up thinking life insurance from day one. When I went to university at Ohio State, my thoughts were that I should go into the accounting field because I was very proficient with numbers—my dad and I used to play number games all the time. But when I took my first accounting course, I said, "Boy, if I have to do this for a living, I am going to die from boredom." So I switched to marketing and economics. Before I graduated, I started interviewing with major industrial companies like IBM and General Motors. I realized very quickly that I would not be happy working for anybody else, and if I really wanted to have the freedom and the success I saw my father and all of his associates have, I needed to be in the insurance business. I graduated on March 16th, got married on March 18th, and started with New York Life on March 27th. I have never looked back.

Why We Endure the Frustrations of the Career

Our industry provides the freedom, the flexibility, and the ability to create a life plan that you can live with forever. But that doesn't mean it is easy. When I first started in the business, even though I had grown up in it, there were things I didn't know. I didn't know how to sell. I understood the mechanics of how things worked, and I understood the technical ways that the split dollar worked, but I had no clue how to present it to individuals so that they could understand it. When you start out in the business, it is very frustrating.

When I first started, I used to think about quitting once or twice a day. Now, after fifty (official) years in the business, I think about quitting only once or twice a month.

It is a tremendous career, but there are still frustrations that we have to deal with. There are still times you scratch your head and ask, "Why am I putting up with this?" Then you sit back and look at the lifestyle you have built for yourself and what you do for your clients, and you say, "Yeah, that's why I am doing this."

How Life Intervened in My Career Path

But there was nothing that was so bad that made me think I should look for another career. Once I started in the career, I saw that there were a lot of career paths available within the industry. One of the things I always enjoyed doing was mentoring people. After a relatively short period of time, two and a half years in the field, I went into the New York Life management program. I was in the program for five years and loved it.

Then my mother became ill with terminal cancer. My dad said, "She's not going to survive. I need you to come back and help me for a while in East Liverpool." New York Life wanted to promote me and give me my own office at that point. Back then, my title was Assistant Manager; today that role is whatever second-line management is. But I took a leave of absence from my management position.

My wife and I had two young children at the time, and we all went back to East Liverpool, Ohio, to help my dad. My mom passed away shortly thereafter. My dad pleaded with me, "Please don't go back to management. I want you to stay here and work with me." That was a very tough decision because my wife and children and I had been living in a community of a million people with all of the amenities that you have in a large community. East Liverpool was a little country town with a population, at that point, of twelve to fifteen thousand. If you wanted to go to a movie, dinner, or shopping, it was all thirty to fifty miles away. It was a tough decision from a lifestyle standpoint, but it was not a tough decision from a career standpoint. I enjoyed what I was doing in management, but I knew that the opportunities of mentoring and working with other people were there as an agent, and my family needed me more than New York Life needed me. So in that respect, working with my father was not a tough decision.

My Advice to Clients: Give Your Advisor Complete Information

The marketing platforms that the industry is using are changing, and companies are finding that to reach certain areas of the market, they have to come up with alternative distribution systems, whether that is with an 800 number, through the Web, or through banks and broker dealers. All of those marketing systems are getting bigger play.

Clients have to understand that when they're sitting down and talking about their financial planning for the next ten to forty years, they have to be very truthful in what they tell their financial advisors because the solutions they get back are only as good as the information they provide. So if clients or prospects don't provide all the information that is pertinent to their particular situation, the solutions they get may not be appropriate for their situation. That is why, when I'm sitting with clients, I make sure they understand that they have to be factual, and they have to be truthful. Maybe there are things that they don't want to divulge that they are embarrassed to talk about or they find it difficult to discuss. I had a client who had disowned one of his children, and he found it very difficult to talk about that. But I needed to know about that so that when we did his estate planning, we had all the information we needed. It is really important for individuals to understand the importance of providing complete and truthful information.

Clients also need to make sure that the individual they are dealing with is not just *hearing* what they're saying, but *listening* to what they're saying. Sometimes somebody will say something, and as you're listening to it, you think, "Okay, this person is telling me something, but he is not telling me everything." You have to ask enough questions to get where you need to go. Clients have to be willing to trust the individual or the system they're using, and they have to be willing to divulge full and accurate information. And they have to be willing to make decisions that are difficult.

My Advice to Agents and Advisors: Make the Calls, Ask the Questions

For financial advisors, the number one priority is that you have to make the calls. Sometimes, an advisor will say to me, "I close every case I work on." My first reaction is, "Well, you're not calling on enough people." Nobody closes 100 percent of their cases—it is not physically possible. In my own career, which was an excellent career, I produced magnificent numbers by anybody's standard, but I still closed only one out of three cases, from the time I opened them until they went full cycle and got paid. And the cases I worked on took six months to a year to complete.

> Nobody closes 100 percent of their cases—it is not physically possible.

So it's the magic of the numbers, making the calls, seeing enough people, and asking enough questions. And you have to ask disturbing questions—the who, what, when, where, and why questions—not ones that clients can answer with a yes or no. You have to listen to what the client is telling you.

You also have to be flexible. For example, if you are going into a client meeting thinking of estate planning, and that client says, "I've already done all my estate planning," you'd better be prepared to go off in a different direction and ask different types of questions. Otherwise, your interview is over. Sometimes I see agents or advisors get so enamored of a particular idea that they will go out and present that idea to a client without ever asking if there is a problem for which that product makes an appropriate solution. Maybe it is a supplemental life insurance retirement plan. The advisor is making a presentation and saying, "Look how good this is" without ever asking, "Does it fit your needs?" So if the person likes the idea, that is one thing, but if the person likes the idea and it has no place in their planning, they are not going to accept it anyway. It is important to ask the right questions to find out what the client's problems and concerns are and be prepared to go off in whatever direction is required to provide the appropriate solutions.

Why Some Companies No Longer Lead with Life Insurance: It is Easier to Talk about Investments than Dying or Becoming Disabled

I think our industry has moved away from focusing on life insurance because it is so much easier to sell non-risk-based products. When advisors or agents call on somebody and say, "I'd like to talk to you about your investments," people are much more receptive than if the advisor says, "I want to talk to you about dying." It's so much easier to talk about investments as opposed to talking about having an illness that will diminish a client's resources or about an accident that might disable them. People don't want to talk about being disabled or dying or having a lingering illness, but they will talk about investments and a higher rate of return and doing better with their money. That's easy to do. It is a much easier sell to make, so the industry has gravitated toward the investment side of the market.

I recently heard a sobering number. The average Merrill Lynch broker generates about $920,000 in commissions per year and only $2,000 in life insurance commissions.

> **It's so much easier to sell stocks, bonds, mutual funds, and other types of products than it is to talk about dying.**

Why is that? Because it's so much easier to sell stocks, bonds, mutual funds, and other types of products than it is to talk about dying, even with people who are the ideal clients to talk to about preserving assets. The way you preserve assets is by proper planning and by securing life insurance to absorb the costs. But people don't want to talk about dying, so advisors don't do it.

Let's Simplify the Paperwork and the Terminology

Looking toward the future, there are a couple of things I think we need to do. One is that we have to get people to come into our industry. We need to attract people to at least consider coming into our industry, and then the industry has to make it easier for them to do their business.

When an agent goes out to see somebody and has to present an illustration that is sixty pages long, followed by an application that is fifteen pages long, followed by a very invasive medical process that might take thirty to ninety days to complete, we put up every roadblock in our industry that we can to make sure somebody doesn't buy.

We, as an industry, have to come up with ways to make it easier to buy. That is what Haven Life has done, and that is what Principal Financial is doing with some of their easy situations—people can get a million dollars' worth of coverage by answering just a few questions. We have to use the prescription drug systems and the MIB (Medical Information Bureau) and avoid doing the medical exams. I think there are so many things that the industry could do going forward, but they have to expedite the field testing and roll it out quicker.

Also, we use terms in our business that don't relate to the consumer, like "death benefit." But what's the benefit of dying? When you talk about a life insurance premium to consumers, they think of a premium-priced product or a premium product in the sense that it is better than everything else. "Premium" does not mean "cost" in the normal sense of the word. So we tell them, "This is the premium," and they don't relate. We need to come up with terminology that is more acceptable to the consumer so that we can get through compliance.

A Haunting But Valuable Lesson I Learned Early in My Career

My father started working with a family back in the 1940s, and my brother and I continued to work with the client. I had done some personal work for one of the family members who had taken over as the CEO of a public corporation. The various family members had a lot of coverage—the patriarch, the son, the daughters, and the grandchildren. We covered everyone and everything.

I had a meeting with the son, who was the CEO, just before he left for a business trip. We discussed getting additional coverage on him and some new coverage on their CFO—a split-dollar type of coverage. The son said, "Okay, we'll take care of my stuff now, but then when I get back from the trip, we will take care of my CFO. Just leave me all the papers. As soon as you get back, I'll call you, and we'll get it done. No problem."

So I left. I went to Florida, where I had a home, for some vacation time. While I was in Florida, I was listening to the news, and I heard about a US Airways plane that crashed while flying into Pittsburgh, Pennsylvania, where my client was. I was thinking, "My client was supposed to be on a business trip. I hope he wasn't on that plane." Shortly thereafter, I got a phone call from the client's father, who told me that his son had been on the plane that crashed. He said, "I need you to come back to Pittsburgh ASAP." I was one of the first people the father contacted to talk about the financial planning and life insurance products we had in place for all the family members.

> I got a phone call from the client's father, who told me that his son had been on the plane that crashed.

Flying back the next day after that plane had just crashed, everybody in our airplane was very quiet as we began to land.

When I talked to the father, he said the many millions of dollars in coverage were going to go to the company, the family, and all the other individuals involved. I was also sitting there thinking, "You know, I have taken care of everybody's planning except the CFO." The CFO had been sitting next to my client on the airplane that crashed. They both died. My client had a lot of coverage, but the CFO had none because it wasn't in force yet. That was a learning process for me—to make sure to push as hard as I can to get the paperwork done and to get the cases bound, just because you never know what's going to happen.

So I did a great job for my client, but I didn't do a great job for his CFO because I didn't push hard enough to get it done. I delivered millions for the CEO's family and zero for the CFO's family. That mistake I made has always haunted me.

CHAPTER 19

ANTHONY M. (TONY) GARCIA

President and CEO

Foresters™

Toronto, Ontario, Canada

Tony was appointed president and CEO of Foresters in May 2014. He has more than twenty-six years of experience in the North American life and annuity industry, most recently as president of Western and Southern Agency Group, part of a Cincinnati-based Fortune 500 diversified family of financial services companies. Previously, he was president and chief executive officer of TIAA-CREF Life Insurance Company. His financial services industry experience also includes executive positions at Allstate, HSBC, and the HealthMarkets life and health subsidiaries.

Throughout his career, Tony has driven profitable growth and implemented transformational change in each of his roles. He brings exceptional visionary and leadership expertise, combined with a commitment to relationship-building and communications skills, to his role at Foresters.

Tony graduated from Delta State University in Cleveland, Mississippi, with a BBA in finance. He earned his MBA from the Kellogg School of Management at Northwestern University.

He serves on the LIMRA LOMA Global Board of Directors, which provides oversight and guidance to LIMRA and LOMA, ensuring that their research and education programs provide value to member companies. He also serves on the Board of Trustees for The American College. He has served on the Board of Directors of the Cary M. Maguire Center for Ethics in Financial Services at The American College and the Board of Directors of the American Council of Life Insurers.

In addition, Tony served on the Cincinnati Chamber of Commerce's Diverse by Design committee, which aims to attract and retain diverse talent to the region. He has been active in the United Way and was a Junior Achievement volunteer teacher.

TONY'S STORY

When I was a junior in college, I took a life insurance class as part of a business-school elective. I was about twenty-one. It was pretty elementary back then—you paid a premium, and there were multiple "flavors." I think taking that class is what eventually led me into the business. I learned about the good that life insurance did and the tax preferences, and it appealed to me intellectually.

I joined Allstate in 1988. The company had multiple carriers, and I liked the people. I delivered my first death-claim check in 1991, and then I delivered my last one in 2010 at St. Jude's Children's Hospital on a product we developed. We had embedded in the pricing a charitable donations rider. One of our brokers helped us develop the product, and his wife died in her early forties. It was a million-dollar face amount. I flew to St. Jude's Children's Hospital and delivered it.

What kept me in the business early on was a sales manager I had back then, Dave Hook. He kept me comfortable with prospecting and appointment setting and all those things that can drive us out of the business. Right when I had reached certain frustration points, he and some agent friends kept me positive and focused on the business when it might have been easier to do something less hard but much less rewarding. Even though the industry offered broader financial services like banking and asset management, I always stayed close to the life insurance business. Ultimately, I reached a career goal—I came to Foresters to run a three-country model that offers life insurance and financial services products in Canada, the United States, and the UK.

Advice to Consumers: Do Your Due Diligence on Your Advisor

A lot of prospective clients will go out on the Internet and get educated, and then before an advisor comes out to meet them, they will at least know a little bit about their options. They want to see if the recommendations the advisor gives them line up with what they're reading online. I would say to consumers, do your due diligence on your advisor. Look for someone you can build a trust-based relationship with, who will meet with you regularly around your financial plan throughout your lifetime, gets industry designations, and commit to

> Do your due diligence on your advisor. Look for someone you can build a trust-based relationship with.

continuous, lifelong learning. Find out how long an advisor has been in the business and what companies he or she represents. And when you're looking for a company, look for a company that is financially strong.

Advice to Agents and Advisors: Surround Yourself with Successful People

The issue of financial transparency is important. The consumers you want to build your business with will be people who ask the right questions. Be proud to tell people how you are compensated and the value you add to their situation.

Our industry is composed of lifelong learners and people who are committed to mentoring others, both formally and informally. Other industries are not as open as we are about sharing ideas and success stories. Take advantage of that. Surround yourself with really successful people who are willing to share their strategies, and build relationships with them. They will tell you anything you want to know.

> No advisor can be all things to all people.

Also, decide where you will devote your focus and passion. Are you going to take care of certain segments? Are there relationships, interests, or causes in your personal life that drive your motivation? I think the most successful people in our business today are those who pick a market niche that plays to their strengths, and that is what they focus on. No advisor can be all things to all people. Not everyone will succeed in the same markets. You can use your prospect-building and relationship-building programs to build a niche in any market using life insurance as a foundation.

The complexity of our business is a blessing. It requires specialization, and we have to we continually sell the value of what we do. Go deep but not wide.

Let's Work Our Way Back to the Foundation of Life Insurance

The business has changed so much since we have been in it. We have fewer life insurers than we did in the past, and in the past twenty years, many carriers have focused on high-net-worth, affluent clients. So one of our challenges is building distribution in the middle market and getting advisors to spend time out there. They aren't sure if they will make money in that market.

Our population is starting to age, and less than 15 percent of all Fortune 500 companies offer a defined-benefit plan. Individuals are having to work their way to funding their retirement. In terms of fundamental, basic life insurance protection, I think many companies have lost their way because it is a difficult product to sell. Both companies and advisors have followed demographic trends that have worked out well for both of us but caused us to take our eyes off the core fact that life insurance is the foundation of any financial plan.

Some advisors have wanted to focus more on the upscale market or get more in the retirement-planning space to increase the prestige of their practices. But many of us have stayed true to life insurance and have been able to carve out niches and still grow while some aspects of the industry have gone south.

We Need to Learn How to Market to Millennial Consumers Effectively

We have a lot of work to do as an industry. And if we do it right, I think that the next generation—my kids—will be a lot more conservative than I was. We need to figure out what is going to drive the Millennials to buy. I think it is more than just the cumbersome underwriting process and buying preferences. A lot of it is the way we explain what we do as an industry and what types of people we put in front of younger consumers. The real challenge with Millennials is that they are going to want to work a different model than what we were raised to do, but they are still going to need advisors. I think we will need a tailored marketing effort to get the next generation to buy our products and to come into our business.

> I think we have made strides in making our product literature understandable for consumers and describing the features and benefits in an effective way.

I am incredibly bullish about the future. We are a fraternal benefit society that's more than 140 years old, so our long-term strategy is focused on how to do a better job in the family market. Member-based organizations like ours have to focus on community building; that helps differentiate us in the marketplace. I am proud of the fact that the incoming generation will be much more thoughtful and conservative with their money. That plays well to our products. I don't think everyone will find a Morningstar Mutual Fund to bet on and never look at it again, like we did until we all woke up years ago. I think we have made strides in making our product literature understandable for consumers and describing the features and benefits in an effective

way. I still think there is way too much "legalese," but I am optimistic that we will be able to work with regulators to make it simpler for consumers to understand what we offer.

I still think the role of financial advisor is a top-rated profession and will continue to be in the next ten to twenty years. As an industry, we have a great story to tell. We need to do a better job of getting advisors to understand consumers and to understand the power of life insurance and how it changes the lives of those customers. I think we are doing a better job on the technology side of the business.

As much as things are changing, I think our success will depend on how carriers and advisors continue to transform themselves to be relevant. I am seeing a lot of positive changes in the business. We are bringing in bright people, both in the field and in the home office. It seems like we're being attractive to some really smart people who really want to make a difference.

Let's Be Evangelists for Life Insurance

The power of life insurance changes lives in a way nothing else can. I knew a young family whose primary income earner died of cancer about fifteen years ago. He had a good advisor and had prepared for the future of his two children—he bought life insurance. When he passed, as tough as that was, the wife and kids were able to go on without having to make any lifestyle changes. The kids recently finished college, and the wife has remarried. They did not see his illness coming. Without the power of life insurance, there is no way their lives would have ended up as well as they have once they lost his income.

We need to get more evangelical about our story.

There aren't many industries that are as noble as ours—maybe teachers, firefighters, and policemen. We need to continue to tell the story in a positive way and not feel the need to be defensive.

CHAPTER 20

THOMAS H. HARRIS,

CLU, CHFC, FLMI

Executive Vice President, Distribution;

Chairman of Hornor, Townsend, & Kent, Inc.

The Penn Mutual Life Insurance Company

Philadelphia, Pennsylvania

Tom, a member of Penn Mutual's Executive Team, is Executive Vice President, Distribution, and Chairman of Hornor, Townsend, & Kent, Inc., a wholly owned broker/dealer subsidiary of Penn Mutual. In these roles, he is responsible for profitably growing Penn Mutual's life and annuity businesses through strong relationships with career advisors as well as independent advisors, who value a direct relationship with the carriers they represent.

Tom leads Penn Mutual's two distribution channels, the Career Agency System and the Independence Financial Network. His additional responsibilities include HTK, contracts, licensing, registration, advisor compensation, annuity distribution, relationship management, professional and practice development, and practice management.

Tom's career spans more than thirty years in all facets of distribution leadership. Previously, as Senior Vice President of Prudential Select Brokerage, he was responsible for growing life insurance sales through independent producers. He joined Prudential Select Brokerage in 2002 as Vice President, Independent Producer Distribution. In 2004,

Tom became Senior Vice President, responsible for Prudential Select Brokerage, where he grew Prudential's share of life business written through Brokerage General Agents.

Before joining Prudential Select Brokerage, Tom was Vice President, Field Sales Support. His team provided advanced marketing, product, and promotional support for Prudential's Individual Life Insurance operation.

Tom is a graduate of Temple University, with a bachelor's degree in actuarial science. He is very active in the industry as a member of the AALU and NAIFA. He has served as chair of the American Council of Life Insurers (ACLI) Distribution Committee, co-chair of the ACLI Producer Licensing Task Force, trustee for The American College, board of advisors for The Penn Mutual Center for Veterans Affairs at The American College, and chair of the LIMRA Brokerage Committee.

TOM'S STORY

How I Went from Loving the Science of the Business to Loving the Passion of the Business

My relationship with life insurance started as more of a fascination more than a love affair back in 1981. I started college thinking I wanted to be a chemical engineer. I went to Drexel for my freshman year, right here in Philadelphia. It is a phenomenal college, and they have great engineering programs. But I found out over the course of that year that I really didn't like chemistry, so being a chemical engineer wasn't really going to work out. I transferred to Temple and took some basic business courses. One of them was an insurance and risk course. In that class, I learned that I could major in actuarial science, so I decided to make that my major. I stayed with it, I loved it, and I ended up getting my actuarial science degree. But by the end of my college career, I knew I didn't really want to become an actuary. However, the education gave me the foundation in terms of understanding the math and science behind the life insurance business. It gave me a foundation upon which I have been able to build a great career.

Then I started my career at Prudential. After a short time, I ended up working in a regional marketing office that supported about three thousand agents, and that is when I went from loving the science of the business to really loving the passion and impact the business has. Working with those agents and field leaders, I started to understand the impact life insurance has on people's lives and on businesses being able to continue after one of the leaders passes. They shared with me how life insurance applies to real-life situations and can have real-life impact. They also shared with me the horrible outcome that can result if somebody doesn't have the right kind of planning and the right kind of insurance in place. I got the opportunity to hear from some industry giants like Sid Freedman, Tom Wolf of FNA, and John Savage. I still remember the edict, "Pay yourself first." I heard from people who really started to open my eyes and ears to the passion, the emotion, and the impact that life insurance can have on people's lives, and how devastating it can be if they don't have it.

"Pay yourself first."

That's the way I went from a fascination with life insurance to having life insurance be a fundamental part of my personal life, my business, and my career.

My Father's Reluctance to Purchase Enough Insurance Deepened My Commitment

The passion I developed for life insurance really became personal for me during the last several years of my father's life. I had coached him into talking to an advisor about life insurance, and he always kind of blew me off. I knew it was the right thing, and I believed that, but I couldn't get him to make that step and sit down with somebody. He got sick the last six years of his life, and he would have been uninsurable. When he passed away, I remember helping my mom go through all of his papers. We found a small group insurance policy he was entitled to, but it was for only $10,000. Fortunately, we weren't left destitute. I didn't have to leave my house, but it was really a missed opportunity for my father to prepare my mother and to prepare things for his grandchildren's future. I realized that he was a great man who was loved by so many, but he had basically no life insurance in place.

> I had coached him into talking to an advisor about life insurance, and he always kind of blew me off.

Not only did I go to school for a career related to life insurance, but I had been working for a life insurance company my whole career. Still, I wasn't able to convince my father to do something that would have been tremendously important to my mom's life and to the lives of the rest of our family members. At that point, I doubled down and really got into sharing with people the impact of life insurance.

You hear these stories about communities or neighborhoods pulling together to host charitable golf tournaments to raise money for kids' college tuition because an income earner has died. And that family is not going to be able to stay in their house or send their kids to college. It is a feel-good story when people rally around a family like that, but when you think of it, at the root of that situation is a missed opportunity. That mom or that dad could have taken control of their financial lives so they wouldn't have to rely on the kindness of neighbors and others. They could and should have been accountable to their family members by purchasing life insurance.

In a nutshell, I couldn't convince my father to do the right thing. So I have tried to spend the rest of my career—not only myself, but through the people I work with—trying to convince others of the importance of understanding what life insurance can do for them and how it's a critical part of a financial plan. That should really be the starting point of your financial plan because it makes every other component work better.

> **Know that you are doing the right thing—you just haven't found the right words to help someone understand yet.**

The situation with my dad wasn't a down note for the rest of my career; it became a driver of continued passion. As you know, you get a lot of rejection in our business, and I think the only way you can sustain an optimistic outlook is to know that you are doing the right thing—you just haven't found the right words to help someone understand yet. And you keep on going at it until they do, hopefully.

Our Job Is to Educate Consumers

I believe that people don't like to face their own mortality, and I think there is a mistaken impression that life insurance is expensive. These are two prongs of a problem that we have in this industry. We need to proactively combat them and educate people because there are fewer advisors today, and more advice is being delivered without some of the emotion, the passion, and the storytelling. A quality advisor is one who has the relevant education, is committed to the career, and continues to learn and improve himself or herself. That is the type of advisor who can really get at the emotions and discover what people think and how they feel.

This type of advisor is empathetic and tells stories that put people in a world that is either so much better than they expect because they have life insurance or makes them face that harsh reality of what their loved ones would go through without life insurance protection.

If you don't plan, it is not going to get any better. As a matter of fact, it could get devastatingly worse. I think it takes a special kind of person to be open to having that conversation with an advisor. Advisors have to be the educators. To do that, they have to be passionate, and they have to believe that it is not about the money; it is about making sure this person they've given advice to and planned for can avoid a catastrophic outcome, either for their business or their family or charities, if they want to continue to support them. That is the issue we face, and frankly, it has been an ongoing battle over the past three decades that I have been in the business. Fewer and fewer people are skilled and able to tell that story, to put themselves in the client's position so they can encourage them to make that decision to buy life insurance and start now. People are losing time as an asset—the longer they wait to get life insurance, the harder it becomes. Get started now!

> **People are losing time as an asset—the longer they wait to get life insurance, the harder it becomes. Get started now!**

Advice to Consumers: Prepare for the Future Now

We all have either a lot of time or a little time, and we don't know which it's going to be, but it's a precious asset, and you want to use it to your advantage. Too often, people don't take advantage of the time they have to properly plan until it's too late. That's true for life insurance and for retirement planning, which probably has more of the media discourse today because in general, people aren't ready for retirement. Well, it's really hard to get ready when you're stepping through that door to retirement. The time to get ready is thirty-five years before it happens. That is when you can use time to your advantage. So use that time to your advantage, and get started now.

Certainly, it is advice that I am giving to my daughter about saving for retirement. She just got married. Whether it is business or my family, I can only provide the advice; I can't make people take it. But working with somebody who is willing to have that conversation is so important.

Robo-Advisors Can Never Replace Financial Advisors

There is a lot of fear about robo-advisors taking over our industry. There's nothing that can take the place of a qualified advisor being able to sit across the table or boardroom with clients, face-to-face, listening to them, reading how they are reacting, having empathy for those folks, and telling stories so that this intangible product can become real to them. That's what an advisor can do; a robo-advisor cannot. The value of personalized advice is not going away. In fact, I think it's going to get even more valuable. That's not only my belief—that's Penn Mutual's belief, and we are committed to growing the number of advisors in our industry.

START NOW

How Company Mutualization Changes the Way We Do Business

If you take a look at what it costs for term insurance today versus what it cost twenty or thirty years ago, it's incredible how much the price has come down. I think, in general, what's happened over the past few decades is that there has been a shift toward products that have easier transaction timelines. There was a shift into the investment business. A lot of our advisors were, at one point, very strong in the life insurance business but now have migrated almost exclusively to an investment practice. And it's not that one is good and the other is bad; it's just that those clients they are giving that investment advice to could absolutely use the same advice about life insurance and what it can do for them.

As the price of products came down, companies didn't have the margin to do the level of training that is needed. So many companies moved away from developing brand-new advisors, particularly those that demutualized and greatly reduced their emphasis on advisor development.

When I started with Prudential back in 1984, we had 25,000 agents in the United States. We had a district operation and what we called an "ordinary operation," but they were all "career agents," as we called them back then. The first seventeen years I was there, Prudential was a mutual company, but for the last eight years I was there, it was a public company. We demutualized at the end of 2001. When I left Prudential, we had just over 2,000 career agents in the United States. We actually had more career agents in Japan than we did in the United States. I think that is a microcosm of what's been happening in the industry. Companies like John Hancock, Met, and others that have demutualized are some big powerhouse brand-name companies that once were really focused on the US life insurance business with sizable career agency systems. Today they all have far fewer career agents than they did before they demutualized.

> **We actually had more career agents in Japan than we did in the United States.**

You are not going to get a quick return on capital building an agency force. It's a much longer process, and therefore I believe much harder to do as a public company. I think a mutual company has the ability to invest and be more patient for a career system to grow and develop.

I want to make this clear: I love Prudential. I was there for twenty-five years, and it is a phenomenal company. My wife and I still own whole life policies from Pru and of course some shares of its stock. It just went through a powerful change in terms of what the management team has to manage to. With a mutual company structure, your primary responsibility is to manage the company for the benefit of the policyholder. In a public company, management's primary responsibility is to drive value to the shareholder. You can have great success in either corporate structure, but that's the starting point in both, and it is a very different starting point. I think that starting point leads to significantly different approaches they have to take to be successful and differences in how success is defined.

I think what you see, then, is that the companies still want to distribute because the leadership in those companies still do believe in the value and the power of life insurance. But how do you distribute it with the structure you have now? In the mutual structure, you would do that by trying to build a very large proprietary agency system and invest in it. In a stock or a public company, you still want to get product to market, but proprietary distribution might be too expensive to develop, so you have to find other means to distribute. That is where you see third-party distribution come online, like a brokerage general agency, a BRAMCO, a Crump, or a LifeMark. So you have a variable-cost distribution model instead of a fixed-cost distribution model. I think that is the core reason for the different approaches that public and mutual companies have in the development of a career-agency system.

A Growing Population Combined with Fewer Insurers = Opportunity

I'm extremely optimistic, and I guess it gets back to the science of our business, but it is certainly about the passion as well. I think of the US population that is growing at a constant rate of almost 1 percent a year, so there is an ever-growing number of people who could be exposed to our product. And there has been a decline in the number of companies selling life insurance. In 2014, there were 830 life insurance companies in this country, compared to 2,337 in 1987, according to the 2015 ACLI Factbook. The number of people employed by life insurance companies in the United States has also fallen. In 1990, the industry had approximately 522,600 employees on its payroll. This figure has steadily fallen every year since and reached 345,800 employees in 2014.[7]

> So we have a growing population and fewer providers.

So many companies have exited the business or merged that the number of players has gone down dramatically from the 1987 peak. So we have a growing population and fewer providers. My belief is that the people in this growing population love their kids and their grandkids, and they want to do right by the employees in their businesses, just like people have in our country for decades. That means they have the need for our product; we just have to be more creative in getting in front of them so that they can understand the impact it can have on their lives.

We can do away with the notion that life insurance is too expensive, or they don't need it now, or they can just wait and get it later, when they really need it. All of those are misperceptions that properly informed, properly advised people who love their families would respond to by doing the right thing, just as they have for years with industry greats like Sid Freedman, John Savage, Maury Stewart, and Phil Richards. Those guys know that when you can get somebody to sit down and listen to their story first and figure out how an advisor can help them, good things happen. We just need to figure that out for today's environment.

---

7 . "Development in the Total Number of Life Insurance Companies in the United States from 1950 to 2014," Statista, The Statistics Portal, http://www.statista.com/statistics/194335/total-number-of-life-insurance-companies-in-the-us/.

CHAPTER 21

CHRISTOPHER M. HILGER

President and Chief Executive Officer

Securian Financial Group

St. Paul, Minnesota

Chris is president and chief executive officer of Securian Financial Group, which consistently ranks among the most highly rated life insurance company groups in the nation. He is also CEO of Allied Solutions, LLC, a Securian subsidiary and one of the largest independent distribution organizations serving the financial institution market.

He began his financial services career in 1987 as vice president of operations at Eldredge Corporations and later served as president and CEO of Eldredge's successor, Allied Solutions. In 2004, Chris joined Securian when it acquired Allied Solutions. He immediately became a member of Securian's senior management team, progressively moving into positions of greater responsibility before being named president in 2012. Chris was named Securian's CEO in 2015.

Chris's collaborative leadership style and broad management experience have contributed to Securian's consistently strong sales, revenue, and earnings results. With almost thirty years of experience in small business and corporate leadership positions, Chris has proven experience in distribution development, mergers and acquisitions, strategic planning, and financial management.

Chris has a bachelor of science degree in finance from Indiana University. He serves on the boards of the St. Paul Foundation and the Minnesota Community Foundation.

CHRIS'S STORY

Coincidences Dating Back to 1880 Show I'm in the Right Place

The truth is, I kind of stumbled into life insurance. For the first seventeen years of my career, I was a partner at Allied Solutions, a large national distributor of insurance products to financial institutions and their customers. While at Allied Solutions, I gained quite a bit of practical experience with property and casualty and group insurance products, but there were few opportunities to distribute individual life insurance. Then, in 2004, my partners and I sold Allied Solutions to Securian Financial Group, a company whose insurance products we distributed.

In the years that followed, I was fortunate to have the opportunity to lead several different Securian businesses. The more I learned about Securian and the range of financial protection products it offered, including life insurance, the more excited I became about a long career with the organization. While being a life insurance executive was not something I intentionally set out to do, it was one of those things in life where you look around and say, "Wow, this is where I'm meant to be. I'm lucky."

> I was surprised when one of my new Securian colleagues shared with me a copy of a 1973 annual report that featured a picture and customer service testimonial from my mother.

This sentiment became even more real when I learned of some of my connections to this new company and its city. I knew my mother had worked in the claims department of Securian for a short time early in her career, but I was surprised when one of my new Securian colleagues shared with me a copy of a 1973 annual report that featured a picture and customer service testimonial from my mother. Every day, I look at that picture of her, now framed and hanging on my office wall. And while I knew that both my parents were born in St. Paul, Minnesota—Securian's headquarters since its founding—I was amazed by the number of distant relatives and longtime family friends I encountered in the community.

My wife and I even discovered that my great-great-grandfather, Christopher O'Brien, was the mayor of St. Paul about the same time Securian was founded in 1880. What an unexpected coincidence.

While I didn't originally plan on working in the life insurance industry, the importance of what we do really resonated with me. I get to see the positive impact we have on people's lives each and every day, and I get to work with some extremely talented and dedicated folks whose values align with mine. What more could someone hope for in a career?

Advice to Consumers and Advisors: Seek Alignment and Simplify

The best relationships are ones that have an alignment of interests. So, if you're a consumer, I recommend that you seek advice from an advisor whose interests and values align with yours. If you do that, I believe the details of the financial-planning process will naturally fall into place.

Likewise, if you're an advisor, intentionally align your professional and personal interests with those of your clients. Work with clients whose values are similar to yours. It is one thing to help reluctant clients make decisions that are in their best interests. It's an entirely different matter (and no fun) to compromise your values just to make a sale.

> **"Is this first and foremost in my client's best interest?"**

Finally, align your financial interests with those of your clients, as much as reasonably possible. Getting a commission on the sale of life insurance absolutely aligns with the security your client receives by purchasing the product. The same is true for most of the other products you sell. Test every recommendation by asking yourself, "Is this first and foremost in my client's best interest?"

This simple question helps our industry make a big impact. We're uniquely positioned to improve lives in ways no other industry can. Only the insurance industry has the combination of product solutions and expertise to help people construct financially secure futures. And it can be complicated.

From young parents to grandparents, homeowners to business owners, people need your help.

While helping your clients with their financial-security needs can be complicated, the industry has a great opportunity to simplify the experience. Let's be honest—life insurance is not always the easiest product to purchase (or sell!). Insurance companies must make the process clearer, faster, and easier. Technology is helping, but there is much more we can do, Simplifying processes will help advisors better educate and guide their clients, leaving them more confident about their own financial futures.

Every Financial Plan Needs Life Insurance

When I was visiting one of Securian's larger distribution firms recently, I was invited to attend a regularly scheduled meeting they call their "All-Hands Meeting." A significant part of the meeting is dedicated to advisors sharing client success stories, with the objective of getting input from peers and ultimately improving prospecting and servicing efforts. While the names of the clients are kept confidential, the advisors are encouraged to offer specifics about clients' financial objectives and personal circumstances.

That day, a newer advisor shared a story about a husband and wife who had completely different attitudes about financial planning. Over the course of several meetings, the advisor was able to gain an understanding of each of their concerns and risk appetites. In the end, the advisor pulled together a financial plan that worked for both of them and incorporated an existing 401(k) account, an individual annuity, and a more appropriately diversified investment account.

When the newer advisor finished telling her story, many of the other advisors praised her for a job well done. She understood the (often conflicting) objectives of the couple and constructed an appropriate financial plan that met those objectives. But one of the more senior advisors in the meeting stood up and asked if the young advisor was open to some feedback. She said, "Sure."

The senior advisor said to her, "You have done such a nice job, but why is there so much risk in your plan?"

She replied, "There's not. I spent time with this couple to understand their moderate risk appetite, and their investment portfolio is absolutely aligned with it."

He said, "I'm not talking about that risk. I'm talking about the risk that your great plan blows up overnight— both the husband and wife are working and in their prime income-earning years. You have done nothing to protect their family, and all of your hard work on their financial plan, if either of them were to die prematurely. Of course, life insurance covers the lives of your clients. But think about it also as insurance for your financial plan. Life insurance *must* be part of your plan."

> "You have done nothing to protect their family, and all of your hard work on their financial plan, if either of them were to die prematurely."

To me, this discussion is a great reminder of how life insurance is much more than a product sale. It's a critical part of a comprehensive solution to make sure your clients, and your plan, are protected. If that's your motivation, how can you *not* talk about life insurance?

An Eighty-Year Policy Demonstrates Four Generations of Teamwork

When reflecting on the main title of this book, "Promises Kept," I couldn't help but recall a story that demonstrates the total team effort it takes to keep the promise of life insurance.

As I mentioned, while I've been in the insurance industry for virtually my entire career, it wasn't until later in my career, the last ten or twelve years now, that I focused on life insurance. Since that transition, I hear on a regular basis the powerful impact that life insurance has on people's lives. Usually it comes in the form of stories from our clients and their families, our distribution partners, and our associates.

At the beginning of every year, one of my colleagues recaps at a senior management meeting some of the life insurance claims Securian paid during the previous year. He provides information on the youngest person we paid a death benefit on, the largest claim we paid, the smallest, and so on. There are always interesting and emotional stories about how the benefits impacted the families of the people who passed away.

One memorable example was a small claim paid on a policy that had been issued eighty years prior.

Think about that. An advisor delivered a promise to a person eighty years ago that most likely concluded with a statement something like: "When your family needs us, we're going to be there." And we were.

The advisor passed away some years later but many years before the insured died. Yet four generations of Securian associates (and six different Securian CEOs) serviced that policy and made sure we were in a position to pay the claim when needed. The collective efforts of so many allowed that fundamental promise delivered by the advisor to be fulfilled eighty years later.

For me, this example highlights the significance of the partnership between the person delivering the promise—the advisor—and the entire team of people across many decades who are counted on to honor the promise. This type of commitment doesn't exist everywhere. We are truly part of a special profession.

CHAPTER 22

GARY "DOC" HUFFMAN,

CLU, CHFC

Chairman, President, and CEO

Ohio National Financial Services

Cincinnati, Ohio

Doc is the chairman, president, and chief executive officer of Ohio National Financial Services. He joined Ohio National in August 2008 as Vice Chairman, Distribution, advancing to Vice Chairman and Chief Operating Officer in 2009 and president and CEO in 2010.

Doc started his career in the insurance business in 1975 as an agent with MassMutual Life and later became a General Agent. He qualified for the MassMutual Leaders Club for twenty years and is a life member of the Million Dollar Round Table.

In 1994, Doc joined MassMutual Insurance Company as Senior Vice President of the Annuity Strategic Business Unit. In 1999, he joined Union Central Life Insurance Company as Senior Vice President, Individual Insurance. In 2008, he was elected president and CEO of the Union Central Life Insurance Company.

Doc serves on the boards of The American College, the Dan Beard Council, Boy Scouts of America, the Cincinnati Opera, Cincinnati Children's Foundation, the United Way of Greater Cincinnati, and Maple Knoll. He is a former chairman of the Life Insurance Marketing and Research Association. A Kentucky native, he is a graduate of the University of Kentucky.

DOC'S STORY

An Opportunity to Start a Business with Someone Else's Money

My father-in-law introduced me to the life insurance business in Memphis, Tennessee. He was in the property and casualty business for his whole career. He had a contemporary, a man by the name of Ewing Carruthers, who worked for MassMutual for more than seventy years. Ewing wrote a book about the life insurance industry in 1969 titled *A Way of Life*. I have that book on my bookshelf that he signed for me and gave to me when I came in the business in 1975.

Milly and I were married after our junior year in college, and as I was getting ready to graduate from the University of Kentucky, Milly's father called me and asked how the job hunting was going. Actually, in a polite way, he was saying, "Now that you've got a college degree, how are you going to support my daughter?"

I told him I was interested in sales, and he said, "Well, if you're interested in sales, you should get in the insurance business."

I said, "You know, Frank, I don't know anything about automobile insurance or homeowner's insurance and all that."

He replied, "No, don't get in the property and casualty business. Get in the life insurance business. It's much more creative; it's much more fun. They do things like estate planning and business continuation planning."

As a twenty-one-year-old kid, I had no idea what he was talking about. But he convinced me to go down to Memphis and meet Mr. Ewing Carruthers. So I went to Memphis on a Friday and had lunch with Mr. Carruthers. He spent three or four hours with me. After I left his office, I knew I was going into the life insurance business, and I knew I was going to join MassMutual. Mr. Carruthers told me about the career and how he kept families together and businesses going.

"Gary, this is an opportunity to start your own business with somebody else's money."

124

I'll have to confess that at age twenty-one, that didn't mean as much to me then, but where he really got my attention was when he said this, with his thick Southern drawl: "Gary, this is an opportunity to start your own business with somebody else's money." He was talking about MassMutual's new-agent financing plan. He said, 'The great thing about this business is that you get paid twice. For every dollar you earn for the first year of commission, there is another dollar waiting for you down the road in the form of renewal commission." He threw out a number and said that whether he worked or not that year, he would make hundreds of thousands of dollars even if he didn't sell a dime's worth of new business. I thought, "Wow, what a business!"

Two Months into My Career, My Passion for Life Insurance Was Born

I didn't really understand the power of life insurance when I first got in the business. But that changed quickly. In my first couple of months in the business, my General Agent said, "Doc, I have an 'orphan' death-claim check." In those days, all the death claims ran through the agency system at MassMutual. He said, "I want you to go deliver it."

I said, "Oh, jeez, Mr. Marcum. I don't know anything about delivering death-claim checks."

He told me, "Oh, you'll learn. Here's the checklist, and here's the fifty-thousand-dollar check. This young widow will be happy to see you."

> So at two months in the business, I got a real passion for the difference we make in people's lives every day because I got to see it applied firsthand with this young widow.

I went to the young woman's house. She was in her late twenties, and she had three children. She was a stay-at-home mom, and her husband had been tragically killed in an automobile accident. I delivered the check, and everything went just fine. When I left to drive back to the office, I felt pretty depressed because it dawned on me—here's a stay-at-home mom with three young children, and all the money she has in the world is $50,000. What is she going to do? But by the time I got back to the office, I realized, what if she had nothing? At least this $50,000 can buy her some time to get herself repositioned. And that's exactly what she did with the money. Her parents helped her out, and she went and got some job training and got a job. Ultimately she remarried, and everything worked out great. Had it not been for that $50,000 she would have been basically without anything. God knows what would have happened to her and her three young children.

So at two months in the business, I got a real passion for the difference we make in people's lives every day because I got to see it applied firsthand with this young widow.

I became pretty passionate about the business. I became a General Agent at age twenty-eight in the MassMutual system, so I had the opportunity to recruit people into the business, train them, and show them what a difference we can make in people's lives. From that point on, I always felt like everyone I met, whether I introduced them to our career or sold to them, was better off after they met me than before they met me. I think most people who have been around the business a long time really feel that way.

Still Making a Difference Twenty Years after the Sale

I have a perfectly balanced career. I was in the field for twenty years as an agent and General Agent, and now I've been on the corporate side for twenty years. Clients still call me—number one, to ask me for advice, and number two, to thank me for what I did with them twenty, twenty-five, or thirty years ago because there have been some deaths in their families. Some people have retired out of pension plans I sold, and some people have gone on disability. In fact, one of the most amazing things to me is that in the past year, four old friends have called me and thanked me for selling them disability insurance because they have been on disability. I didn't even know it because I don't live there anymore.

When I was selling life insurance, I had a client who had a family business, a manufacturing operation. The family desperately needed to buy life insurance to fund their buy-and-sell operation. They also needed life insurance to pay the estate tax bill when the patriarch and the matriarch of the family died. But I couldn't get them there. This case went on for four or five years. One day, I was having lunch with the son, one of the children, who was the general manager. His parents were on a business trip. I said to him, "John, can your family afford another four to five million dollars' worth of debt?"

He said, "No. We would have to sell assets—we couldn't afford that."

I told him, "Look, heaven forbid the plane crashes with your parents coming home from their trip, that's what you're going to have to do within nine months to pay the estate tax bill."

Now, this was a case where their lawyer, their accountant, and their trust officer all agreed that the insurance was needed. Everybody was in agreement, but I couldn't get them to move. I wasn't getting through to him. This estate tax business was just something that was just out there; it wasn't really real. But what was real to John was debt service. He understood that. So when I put it in terms that he could understand, within thirty days, we had this case done. It was one of the biggest cases I had sold at that point in my career.

Unfortunately, John's wife had cancer and died a couple of years ago. A few months before that, his mother died. Milly and I went down for his wife's visitation because we were good friends with them. As I was going through the receiving line to speak to the family, I saw John. As I was consoling him about the death of his wife, I was getting ready to leave and he said, "Oh, Doc, do you have a second?"

> We had set out this plan fifteen or twenty years earlier, and now it was coming to fruition. And he felt it was important to thank me, even in his time of grief.

I said I did. He told me, "I meant to say this to you when I first saw you. I can't tell you how much that planning meant to our family when my mother died a couple of months ago. I want to thank you for what you did for our family."

There was a person in grief who just lost his wife and lost his mother a couple of months earlier. We had set out this plan fifteen or twenty years earlier, and now it was coming to fruition. And he felt it was important to thank me, even in his time of grief. It just shows the power of what we do and the effect we have on people's lives and on their families.

Any person who gets the opportunity to experience the difference we make in people's lives firsthand—how could they not be passionate about what we do? It changes people's lives.

Advice to Consumers: Focus on the Benefit of Life Insurance, Not the Cost

Like most new life insurance agents, I bought life insurance when I came in the business. So I have some forty-year-old life insurance policies with a mutual company, and it is the best single asset I own—cash on cash. And that doesn't even include the death-benefit protection it provides for Milly and our family in my estate.

There is not a better asset you can own than permanent whole life insurance.

Now, while I own everything from the companies I have been with—manufactured BUL/UL, everything—the design share of my program is good old whole life insurance. My advice for consumers is that you need to take the time to understand how this fabulous financial product works because I have lived it. I have seen what it can do. I think the mistake people make many times is focusing on the cost and what it looks like, not what we want it to accomplish.

Everything I have ever promised when I sold a whole life insurance policy—to myself and to the people I was fortunate enough to serve—has all come true. I can't say that about any other financial product I've sold in my forty years in the business.

Advice to Agents and Advisors: Learn How Life Insurance Works

My advice to financial advisors is to know that the game is changing. It's unfortunate to me that whole life insurance is just not sexy. But given what's coming down the pike with this new DOL fiduciary standard, I think that ironically, it will have a positive effect on new advisors coming into the business. I think it will drive new advisors to sell more life insurance instead of mutual funds and variable annuities. My advice for financial advisors today is to understand how life insurance works. If selling whole life insurance is not a huge part of your practice, then you are doing a great disservice to your clients.

> If selling whole life insurance is not a huge part of your practice, then you are doing a great disservice to your clients.

If you're interested in doing the right thing by your clients, you owe it to them to teach them about the power of whole life insurance. All this other stuff is fine, but without whole life insurance, people don't have a complete plan, in my opinion.

Why the Focus Has Shifted Away from Life Insurance

Investment products are a much easier sale than life insurance, and people want to talk about assets under management but not their mortality.

Now, in fairness, I have variable annuities. I have an old defined-contribution pension plan that I sold to myself when I was a General Agent. I have done all the things that any financial planner would do, but I always made sure that the base and the foundation of my financial plan was whole life insurance. That's because if something happened to me, none of the planning I did would come to come to fruition without life insurance.

Let's Hope We Never Experience This Again

But as we have progressed along, the world has changed. Beginning in the early 1980s, I had a thirty-year fixed mortgage with 13.5 percent interest. You couldn't go down any street or highway without seeing a billboard with a bank advertisement that said, "If you'll put $1,500 in an IRA every year for thirty years, you'll be a millionaire." They were compounding at a crazy rate like 15 percent.

What came out of that high-interest-rate environment was something I believe was really detrimental to the insurance industry: universal life.

The reason it was detrimental was not because of the product, but what happened because of the design of the product. Here's what I mean. All of a sudden, we started recruiting, and we created a generation of producers who didn't know how to fact-find and uncover needs. They built their practices on showing universal life with a 12 or 15 percent interest rate. Of course, the computer and the online sales illustrations that became prevalent in those years helped all this—advisors became spreadsheet artists and replacement artists. And so we began to create a generation of salespeople who really didn't understand how to sell life insurance.

Then we went from there to the greatest bull market we've ever seen. I remember that when I went into MassMutual's home office, I had the annuity business. I told our president at the time, "You know what's going to happen? We're going to sell more variable life in the industry than any other product." And that's exactly what happened in 1994 or 1995.

So all of a sudden, we went from this high-interest-rate environment and the creation of universal life to now, when we're in the variable world. Again, people are spreadsheet artists. We continue to get away from selling life insurance, fact-finding with people, and talking about their dreams and aspirations.

Let's Get Back to the Basics

My hope is that we can get back to the basics and start talking about insurance again and helping people understand it. We need to teach advisors how to get prospects, fact-find, develop the need, and solve the needs people have.

When I was at Union Central, one of our agents in Memphis, Tennessee, a guy by the name of Bobby Brown, invited me to speak at an annual meeting of the NAIFA board when he was the NAIFA president. He wanted me to talk about the evolution of the insurance business from my perspective. I told him I would be happy to do that. I said, "Look, I'm somewhat biased, and everybody may not agree with me, but I will give you my personal opinion." He wanted me to address it from the historical perspective first. I said, "Look, I go back to when I came in the business in 1975. What was I basically selling? Whole life, term, and disability. I didn't even have a securities license, so I wasn't selling any variable annuities. I did sell a fixed annuity from time to time. But my focus was really on selling whole life insurance. And for people who were on a budget, we would sell term first and convert it over time. It was a pretty simple approach back in those days.

> There are only two ways to make money—a person at work or capital at work.

It goes back to all those things Mr. Carruthers used to talk to me about years ago. I think we have a ton of people still in the business today who really don't know how to do what those of us who have been in the business a long time know what to do.

As we move forward, let's return to what has always worked well—making life insurance the foundation of every financial plan.

CHAPTER 23
ROBERT R. JOHNSON,
PHD, CFA, CAIA

President and CEO; Professor of Investments

The American College

Bryn Mawr, Pennsylvania

Bob has served as president and chief executive officer of The American College of Financial Services since October 2014. He also is a professor of investments. His areas of expertise include executive compensation, financial planning, investments, portfolio management, and security analysis.

Prior to joining The College, Bob served as professor of finance in Creighton University's Heider College of Business. From 1996 to 2011, he held a number of senior executive positions at CFA Institute. He has extensive experience with credentialing programs, ethical and professional codes of conduct, and global business expansion.

Bob is the author of multiple books and more than seventy scholarly articles. He is the coauthor of the books *Invest with the Fed, Strategic Value Investing, The Tools and Techniques of Investment Planning*, and *Investment Banking for Dummies*. He has published in the *Journal of Finance, Journal of Financial Economics, Journal of Portfolio Management, Financial Analysts Journal,* and *Journal of Investing,* among others. He also serves on the editorial board of the *Journal of Portfolio Management.*

Bob has extensive media relations experience and has been quoted in many publications, including *The Wall Street Journal*, *Financial Times*, *Barron's*, and *Forbes*. He has appeared on many televised shows and networks, including ABC World News, Bloomberg TV, and CNN.

He is the recipient of the 2013 Alfred C. "Pete" Morley Distinguished Service Award from CFA Institute, the Robert F. Kennedy Memorial Student Award for Teaching Achievement (Creighton University), and Outstanding Faculty Member of the Year Award at Creighton for three years.

From 2012 to 2015, Bob served on the board of RS Investment Management.

He holds the CFA charter, the CAIA charter, a BSBA degree from University of Nebraska–Omaha, an MBA from Creighton University, and a PhD from the University of Nebraska–Lincoln.

BOB'S STORY

A Career Devoted to Financial Services Education

I think it is inaccurate to say that I have a love affair with life insurance. I have a love affair with the financial services profession. I actually had very little relationship with the life insurance profession before becoming president of The American College of Financial Services in October 2014. I have come to really admire the life insurance profession and feel privileged to have gotten to know and work with some of the real giants in the profession through my affiliation with The American College of Financial Services.

> I believe that the level of financial literacy is highly correlated to financial security and is a major determinant of quality of life for many individuals and economies.

My entire career has been devoted to financial services education. Financial literacy and financial security are extremely important to me. I believe that the level of financial literacy is highly correlated to financial security and is a major determinant of quality of life for many individuals and economies.

I was fortunate at an early age to be exposed to the importance of financial planning. I came from a very middle-class background and watched my parents struggle from paycheck to paycheck. I realized that I didn't want to suffer that same fate and that financial education was the key for me to make my own future.

I had the great fortune of attending high school with Warren Buffett's son, Peter. That led me to an awareness that there were people like Mr. Buffett who made a living in the investments profession. Later on, when choosing a major in college, I realized that a life in financial services was a possibility.

"Pracademia": The Sweet Spot between Academia and Practice

I also decided to focus my career on the intersection between academia and practice—a space I like to call "pracademia." I believe that to a large extent, academic business schools have lost their way. Many professors act as if business is a theoretical discipline and not applied as it is. Now, not all business schools operate that way. I was fortunate to be affiliated with Creighton University, which has adopted a very applied view of education. I believe that The American College is a perfect place for me, as we operate in that sweet spot where academia intersects with practice.

By the way, I think we sell ourselves short by referring to life insurance as an "industry." If we want to be seen as the professionals that we are, we need to refer to life insurance as a "profession." Professionals work in a profession. Using the term "industry" denigrates what is a noble profession.

Advice to Consumers: Start Working with an Advisor Early in Your Career

Establish a relationship with a trusted advisor early in your working career. The decisions you make very early in your working career are the most critical decisions to your financial security throughout your life, and ultimately a big determinant in your quality of life. None other than Nobel laureate Albert Einstein was rumored to have said, "Compounding is the most powerful force in the universe." Whether he said it or not is irrelevant. The truth is that people should operate as if he said it. Failing to plan and save early in one's life can have serious negative ramifications later in life. Said positively, a few good decisions early in life can be critical in improving quality of life throughout one's lifetime.

> A few good decisions early in life can be critical in improving quality of life throughout one's lifetime.

Advice to Agents and Advisors: Continue Your Education

There continue to be so many changes in the financial services profession. Your true "value add" is that you can help clients navigate the increasingly complex financial landscape. You cannot assume that what you learned yesterday is "best practice" today. Henry Ford once said, "Anyone who stops learning is old, whether at twenty or eighty."

The financial services profession is evolving rapidly. Advisors who don't continue their education are doing a disservice to clients. For example, in the area of retirement income planning, there have been enormous changes due, for instance, to a low-interest-rate environment and increasing longevity of retirees. Some advisors continue to operate as if the "4 percent rule," for instance, is sacrosanct. New research, some coming from Professor Wade Pfau at The American College, has challenged the 4 percent rule and has shown that in the new environment, retirees run an increasing risk of outliving their assets.

If anyone is in this profession simply to make a living, they are in the wrong profession. The giants in the profession recognize that providing financial security for clients is a calling, not a job. They recognize it as a profession. People in it to simply line their own pockets likely view it as an industry. To understand that, you have to have only one client whose life was changed because someone they loved had life insurance. I don't get tired of hearing the testimonials from people whose lives have been changed—whose kids were able to go to college, whose spouse was able to live his or her life out with dignity—because someone they loved had the foresight to purchase life insurance and because someone counseled them to purchase that life insurance. That is a noble calling.

Also, focus on holistic financial planning. Life insurance is extremely important, but it is but one aspect of a holistic financial plan that includes all of a client's financial and human capital assets. Advisors who concentrate on only one aspect of financial services will, in my opinion, become obsolete. I believe it is akin to a golfer who is a terrific driver of the golf ball but can't putt.

Great Minds Are Just One Reason for Optimism for the Future

I think more than ever, truly remarkable people with terrific minds are devoting their careers to the financial services profession. Much of the research being published today will positively influence people's future quality of life. I am energized being around really bright, terrific faculty at The College—people like Wade Pfau, Jamie Hopkins, David Littell, Craig Lemoine, and others—who have devoted their careers to teaching advancements in financial services and ultimately improving the quality of life of advisors' clients.

⌛ CHAPTER 24

JOSEPH W. JORDAN

Inspirational Speaker and Author

Greater New York City Area

Joe is an independent consultant and author who speaks to myriad groups worldwide. He has a relentless ambition to inspire as many financial professionals as possible with his distinguished presentations and advocacy programs. As a motivational speaker, Joe has spoken at hundreds of events since 2004, including major conferences for companies such as MDRT, GAMA International, NAIFA, and The American College. He has presented in countries including Australia, Japan, India, Greece, Italy, Brazil, and Canada. His presentation, titled "Get Inspired," is specifically tailored to each audience he is speaking to.

With more than forty years of experience in the insurance and financial services industry, Joe's career has spanned every facet of the business, from insurance to annuities to Wall Street.

He began his career with Home Life Insurance Company in 1974. After managing insurance sales at PaineWebber, he joined MetLife to build its annuity business. Later he was responsible for all MetLife retail product development, initiating fee-based financial planning. Joe also founded the Behavioral Finance Organization at MetLife. After holding the position of senior vice president at MetLife, Joe turned his focus to sharing his inspirational message with financial professionals around the world.

In 2011, *Financial Advisor Magazine* honored Joe's book *Living a Life of Significance* as one of its top five books of 2011. In 2015, he released an audiobook program titled *Living a Life of Significance: A Woman's Perspective.*

Joe is a founder of the Retirement Institute, formally known as the National Association for Variable Annuities (NAVA). He is a member of the Fordham University Football Hall of Fame and played rugby for the New York Athletic Club for more than thirty years.

You can read more about Joe at www.joejordan.com.

JOE'S STORY

It Took Me Thirty Years to Realize the Significance of My Own Story

In 1952, my mother was widowed when I was six months old, and I had three siblings. My mother was not a professional person. Before he died, my father cashed in a sizable life policy so he could make an investment. My mother woke up with four kids who had to raise themselves. I have one brother and two sisters, so it was mostly a maternal household. My whole life was built around the idea of the consequences of not having insurance.

I got involved with life insurance in 1974, and at the time, it was just a job. Being very ambitious, I wanted to make sure I became as successful as possible. It was all about me and being aggressive, and I didn't make a personal connection to it. So for my first thirty years in the business, I never used my personal story because I didn't think it was relevant or professional.

In 1974, the world turned upside down. We had the oil embargo, inflation came in big time, and the traditional life insurance products were not built around all of that. I really wanted to be a cool guy, so I wanted to be in the investment business. I think many of us did that. There was a period of time when people in the business didn't really want to be in the business. As a result of that, I went to PaineWebber. I went to Wall Street and thought that was a great move. I got stock brokers to do insurance business, but more on an investment angle and less on the protection side. So I originally saw insurance as a business, a career, and a job. It wasn't a passion for me; it was the way I could put myself forward.

As I began to give speeches, I finally made the connection that if my mother had had the $100,000 policy in force in 1952 when my father died—if he hadn't cashed it in before he died—what would have happened? In 1952, $100,000 was a lot of money. In fact, you could buy a house for $5,000 back then and probably sell it for $300,000 in 1980, when inflation was so high. Finally, it began to dawn on me how much different my mother's life would have been if she had had that money. She worked herself very hard. She became disabled, and my wife and I took care of her in an apartment with two kids. I never made the connection that perhaps my mother felt that her independence and dignity were gone because her legacy was one of dependency on her children.

> Finally, it began to dawn on me how much different my mother's life would have been if she had had that money. She worked herself very hard.

It's Not About Us; It's About the People We Serve

So all of a sudden, when I was in my fifties, for the first time, I could finally relate on a very personal level about the impact insurance would have had on my family. It wasn't a case study or an abstract concept; it was my family. As I spent more time on Wall Street, I saw that the brokers focused on performance. In fact, the way they would differentiate themselves would be something like this: "Do business with me, and I'll select the right investments and time you out of them at the right time to give you the best performance." If you say that or intimate that you will build a referral-free practice, there is no statistical evidence for the persistence of performance. Sooner or later, someone else will claim they can provide the best performance, and the client goes on the gerbil wheel to nowhere in search of that which no one can provide. The producer has to rebuild his or her book. The only thing a producer has a possibility to control is his or her client's behavior. That comes from creating a trusted relationship!

> We, as an industry, have created many self-inflicted wounds in our relationship with the public. Why do you think that recently five countries did away with commissions?

Problem is, we have never been more needed and less trusted because our culture focused more on product features. We put emphasis on what we thought was important. Our metrics measured assets under management and commissions, not benefits. We sold what we knew and were comfortable selling rather than thinking about taking care of people's total needs. We, as an industry, have created many self-inflicted wounds in our relationship with the public. Why do you think that recently five countries did away with commissions? As of this writing, the Department of Labor (DOL) is attempting to create onerous rules in an attempt to legislate ethical behavior.

It's because we are not trusted. The unfortunate consequence of the DOL rule is that it will push professional advice up to the wealthy. This is the unintended consequence of these unwise regulations that will help fuel greater income inequality that we keep hearing about. This is what happened in the UK when similar rules were put in place in January 2013. Parliament is now dealing with the advice gap.

When my career was just starting in 1974, the business was going through rapid change. Significant inflation and high interest rates were rendering the standard product lines obsolete. There was a concerted effort to become more left-brain and analytically positioned. We thought the facts would cover it; there wasn't much emotion tied to it. In fact, in financial services during the time, emotion was looked down on. That's ridiculous because how do you take the emotion out? That's the way people make decisions. Facts are facts, and when you stick to the facts, the facts don't stick because people get emotionally involved. It's really about how you create relationships with people. The fundamental issue is the idea of creating trust so that when you say something, people are not thinking there is something in it just for you; they know you're really concerned about them. This sounds kind of fundamental, but it's back to the basics.

> The fundamental issue is the idea of creating trust so that when you say something, people are not thinking there is something in it just for you; they know you're really concerned about them.

Why should a successful advisor whose income is already more than enough for this stage of his or her career continue to promote, educate, and implement life insurance? It's because clients need it. My income needs might be met, but maybe my client's needs aren't met. We did the research, and we found out that everyone dies.

Having a Diverse Revenue Stream Benefits Everyone

There are times when the stock market goes down or interest rates decline, so diversification makes sense for companies and individuals. There are also regulatory risks. The recent rule changes by the DOL also provide a real incentive to look at protection products. Diversification also benefits clients—it means you're taking care of their multiple needs. Any investment program collapses if someone dies or gets disabled and they have no insurance. And even though selling insurance is not the sexiest thing to do, it is something people really need. Again, it's not about us—it's about the people we serve.

Because it's not as sexy and not as much fun to sell insurance products, a lot of people in financial services and in the insurance business gravitated more toward the investment side. That is not a bad thing to happen because you have to take care of multiple needs, but if you leave life insurance out of the picture, you're leaving a huge gap in terms of taking care of people's real needs.

> If you leave life insurance out of the picture, you're leaving a huge gap in terms of taking care of people's real needs.

Our Biggest Threat Today: The World's Aging Population

The defining issue of the twenty-first century is not terrorism, global warming, or an energy shortage. These are the disaster issues that pop up all the time, and we figure out ways to solve them. The new threat we face is the aging population of the world. People are living a lot longer than they used to. By 2050, there will be two billion people on the planet over the age of sixty. There will be five countries that have more than fifty million people over the age of sixty: China, India, the United States, Indonesia, and Brazil. By 2050, Japan will lose 18 percent of its population, and by the end of the century, it will lose half of its population. China will get old before it gets rich, and by 2050, the country will have about a 20 percent decline in its working-age population. A lot of that came from the one-child policy, so you'll notice that they reversed that. By contrast, the United States will have a 10 percent increase in its working-age population!

> It gets back to the idea of creating fundamental relationships with people and building trust—and no one is better at building trust than women.

The thing about people living longer is that, for the most part, a lot of people don't live healthily. Government programs and corporate pension plans don't support healthy living. When people my parents' age were working, if you picture a pyramid, the base of their pyramid for their financial stability was pensions. The next biggest retirement-income source was Social Security, and then at the top, they might want to invest to supplement those income sources.

Now that pyramid is upside down because pensions are very rare these days, and Social Security isn't enough to support people through their retirement. So they have to be able to invest to take care of themselves.

They have to protect themselves. As Nick Murray says, it's YOYO: "You're On Your Own."

People in financial services, whether they are in the insurance business or at Merrill Lynch, have to understand—and consumers have to understand—that they have to take care of themselves. The sound foundation of any financial plan is to make certain that people are adequately protected because no one else can take care of them. And now people are living longer.

Our business has gone through some changes, and now is the time to focus on the aging population of the world. One of the things that is our prowess is that we provide people independence and dignity in a life span that's never been this long. That's a fundamental issue. To a large extent, I think the way we recruited people in the past was all about money—how much money you will make and the great trips you'll go on. I think we've gotten hard core. In fact, I will tell you that at PaineWebber, the culture was "yield to broker," or YTB. What that meant was, how do I make money on this thing? We never really focused on the client's needs. That's the reason we have all this compliance and why we have this Department of Labor proposal popping up, because people don't really trust us. We became obsessed about ourselves.

We Need to Attract Young People and Women into Our Industry

I think two fundamental changes need to happen in the future. One is that we need to learn how to attract the Millennial group. You will notice that we tend to have an older sales force because the career wasn't attractive to younger people. They are less interested than previous generations in making a lot of money. They want to have a positive impact on the world, and that's what we do. I think we have to emphasize that more often.

The second thing is that feminization of the business is crucial. Women instinctively create relationships. We have gravitated out of the transactional one sitting per client, one sale made, trying to make it simple. We have gravitated more toward a planning paradigm, and that's important. The future doesn't belong to the people with all the answers; it belongs to the people who can ask the right questions. Clients can talk about the past and the present, but they have great difficulty trying to focus in on the future. By asking them the right questions, we can provide clients with added value. It's invaluable for people to have a third party help them begin to envision what the future can be like. The questions should be designed not to sell, but to understand clients' needs.

> It gets back to the idea of creating fundamental relationships with people and building trust—and no one is better at building trust than women.

Advice to Agents and Advisors: Know That You Make a Difference

Approximately 80 percent of the people who enter this business fail—not because they don't know enough or they are insecure about not knowing all of the right stuff. What happens is they just can't take the rejection. That's why we need to reinvigorate all the financial services, especially our business. In the insurance business, you are important and valuable because you can be the most important person in someone's life. As a result of your actions, you can make sure a family is financially secure and make sure a legacy is spawned as a result of what you do. Anyone who meets with you will be better off as a result.

Our business has so much rejection and negativity in it that self-driven motivation isn't enough. What you have to do is be inspired. And if you're inspired to know that you do something worthwhile, you will be able to get through that rejection and to know that you can get through to people.

I think that if we begin to build our businesses based on trust in relationships, then people will respond, and the people in the business will succeed.

I think we have to create a culture that celebrates the impact we have on others, not just how much money you'll make and what the new product is. You have got to not only know it; you have got to believe it. Beliefs drive your behaviors and your desires, your goals. If your goals don't sync with your beliefs, you will always manifest your beliefs.

> **If it's all about you, you will get worn down. But if what you are doing is for a greater purpose, it will energize you.**

If you don't believe you can do something significant and worthwhile, you can be subject to something I know nobody talks about in financial services—low self-esteem. If it's all about you, you will get worn down. But if what you are doing is for a greater purpose, it will energize you. Nelson Mandela said that the only way that people can perform beyond what they think they are capable is through inspiration. And that inspiration comes from helping others.

How do you want to be remembered? When you build a business that enables you to protect others, and then when a family winds up with a crisis, you're the person who walks in and makes it right. It's just a marvelous way to live.

Let's Create a Culture That Builds Advisors' Self-Esteem

You have to think of a person as a whole entity. Our culture cannot be about the next trip or how much money you make, but also about the impact you have on others. I think that's the thing that will allow advisors to continue to prospect.

> The is whether or not people prospect.

I think our culture has to raise people's self-esteem and give people the courage to do prospecting. We create a lot of good, and there is no other business that makes the kind of impact we do. I have some videos that chronicle the story of a Chinese woman who lives in New York. One of her clients had terminal cancer and went back to China to die there. But her particular policy had one of those predeath benefits. So all of her care was being provided for her, and her family didn't have to sell the house. On her deathbed, the last person she thanked was her insurance agent. Now, I guarantee you there is no case in history in which someone on their deathbed thanked their broker for beating the S&P by four basis points. Again, we need to celebrate the significance of what we do and the impact we can have on others. That is essentially what life is all about.

Our culture needs to remind us of our obligations to others. That's one thing MDRT does, and that's why it's important for advisors to qualify for Million Dollar Round Table. In their meetings, they talk not only about sales ideas; they also discuss our impact on others. Another great resource is the Life Happens videos. People should take the time to watch them.

Let's Become "Firms of Endearment"

From a business perspective, the misconception of capitalism is that everyone's in business just for the short term and to make profits. A lot of companies are dominated by finance people who have a very short time horizon and are always looking to maximize profits. The companies that are most profit-driven—and this goes beyond insurance—are never the most profitable because they have forgotten what their purpose is.

The companies that really succeed are the companies that understand their purpose, and then the money comes. So money isn't first; benefit is first. Money comes later.

In the 2014 book *Firms of Endearment*, the authors define a "firm of endearment" as a company that is organized around something other than just making money. They talk about purpose and meaning and the importance of aligning all the efforts of a company's stakeholders, employees, suppliers, clients, and shareholders. It is sometimes harder for public companies to do this. They get pressure from Wall Street analysts who are interested only in short-term results. Employees are overhead, suppliers should be squeezed, and clients tolerated. Said another way, they are chasing the money. A purpose-driven organization and individual always outperforms a profit-driven one.

> A purpose-driven organization and individual always outperforms a profit-driven one.

The book mentions an analysis that was conducted from 1998 to 2013, and the S&P was up 5.1 percent, but it was up 21 percent for the firms of endearment. So the companies that recognize that they exist for the purpose of doing good for others deal with quality versus just price. They are the ones that succeed, and that's how you make the money. That's how you turn it into a benefit to others.

I also think we monitor the wrong metrics. Most of the metrics we measure ourselves on are commissions and assets under management. Seldom do you see any celebration around the face amounts that are created.

One of our top producers at MetLife is doing $2 million in commissions, so he's rather successful. But he wanted to quit the business; he just couldn't take it anymore. He called me up and said, "Joe, I read your book. I finally realized that if all my clients died last night, the greater Philadelphia area would receive more revenue than if it hosted the Super Bowl." He had $1.8 billion of insurance in force, but he never viewed it that way. He never saw the significant impact he is making in people's lives. *When you change the way you see things, the things you see change.*

CHAPTER 25

ROBERT A. KERZNER,

CLU, CHFC

President and CEO
LIMRA, LOMA, and LL Global, Inc.
Windsor, Connecticut

As president and CEO of LIMRA, LOMA, and their parent organization, LL Global, Inc., Bob leads the world's largest association of life insurance and financial services companies. In 2010, he led the merger of LIMRA and LOMA, which together represent more than 1,200 members across sixty-four countries, including most of the world's largest life insurance companies. As the trusted source for industry knowledge, financial services companies look to LIMRA and LOMA for their research, training, and development needs. Under Bob's leadership, LIMRA and LOMA have exhibited record growth and profitability.

Before joining LIMRA in 2004, Bob was executive vice president and head of the individual life division of Hartford Life, Inc. Under his leadership, the division experienced dramatic growth and record financial performance. Bob also led The Hartford into affiliated distribution with the acquisition of Woodbury Financial Services, a national broker-dealer organization with more than 1,800 independent representatives. Bob served as president of Woodbury following the acquisition. His career with The Hartford spanned thirty years, from 1974 to 2004. In his first twenty years, he established performance records in field sales and management before moving into senior management.

A leading voice in the life insurance, retirement, and financial services industry, Bob recently spoke at events held by the Department of Treasury Federal Insurance Office (FIO), the National Association of Insurance Commissioners (NAIC), and Life Insurance Commission of New York (LICONY). He is regularly sought out by leading national publications like *The Wall Street Journal*, *Bloomberg*, and *USA Today*, as well as a host of trade and other business media outlets, to provide insight into industry issues and trends.

Bob is a graduate of Central Connecticut State University.

BOB'S STORY

I Wanted to Do Anything But Sell Life Insurance

My relationship with life insurance certainly was not love at first sight. When I graduated from college, I actually said I would do anything but sell life insurance. It was the only career that I had a definitive idea that I would not do. Oddly enough, someone recruited me from Hartford, but it didn't strike me at the time as pure selling of life insurance because the property and casualty agent had high-end, wealthy business clients. And if you could convince that person to take you out and work with his clients, you could get to a much higher-end client, and you didn't have to do the prospecting.

As a twenty-three-year-old, it wasn't easy to convince the fifty-something-year-old producers to take me out to see their best clients. But once I got involved in it, I realized just how big the need was.

Many of those people were extraordinarily successful and wealthy businesspeople, but they really didn't understand why they should have life insurance. The ability to help them really became fascinating, especially when we got more into helping them pass their businesses to the next generation and doing fairly complex planning with them.

Helping People Is the Greatest Reward

As you know, you have to have a certain skill set to be successful in sales. So while I thought I would never want to do this because the rejection would be too difficult, I found that I was well-suited for it and that, in fact, I could deal with the rejection. But I could also help convince people that they had a real problem when frankly, at times their attorneys and other trusted advisors could not convince them that there was a business solution.

I found that my core skill set of tenacity and persistence really worked well in this career. I also liked feeling that what I was doing made a difference. I wasn't sitting behind a desk all day, and I was doing something that really mattered. I enjoyed helping protect people, whether it was having enough cash to protect their business or protecting their estate so their hard work didn't all go away at their death.

Advice to Consumers: An Advisor Can Help You Make Better Decisions

For the consumer, I think there are two issues. We know from our data that the number one thing people are concerned about is retirement, yet we know that they are not saving enough. Most tell us they know they should save more, but they don't.

At the same time, we know that a record number of people, about 50 percent, say, "I know I need more life insurance." But they don't buy it.

In both cases, what I know is that people make bad decisions. They don't always do the right thing. And frankly, in most cases, when they are confused and when they aren't sure what the absolute perfect decision is, they do nothing. So ultimately, my advice over the years hasn't changed. First and foremost, find a good advisor who can help you really understand what you need and why you need it. Our research has shown that advisors who understand and integrate the tenets of behavioral economics into their presentations are much more likely to help their clients make better decisions. We know we shouldn't eat fatty foods, and we know we shouldn't eat as much chocolate as we like, but that doesn't stop us. That is why obesity is at all-time high in America. We know what we should do, but without someone to help us, we don't do it. That is why people do better when they have coaches and advisors. They need us to help coach them on their financial matters to help them make better decisions.

Advice to Agents and Advisors: Adapt to Change

For advisors, above all, the world is changing, and over the next decade, it is going to change tremendously and incredibly fast. There are going to be profound changes to the business, predominantly caused by regulatory change, as well as by the effects of technology and creating new business models. Advisors need to be flexible. They have to be able to adapt better than ever before, and above all, embrace change. Don't fight it. Look at how to use new capabilities and things that are emerging, like robo-advice and social media. To really leverage these things, don't see them as competitors. Instead, ask, "How do I work these into my practice to make me even better?"

> Advisors need to be flexible. They have to be able to adapt better than ever before, and above all, embrace change.

Advisors also need to know that today's consumer is very different, and you need to work with those consumers in very different ways than you did in the past. Even Boomers are acting different in retirement than they did previously, and certainly different than previous generations. Understanding their goals, challenges, and expectations in *all* aspects of their lives will help you develop financial plans and provide advice that will serve them well. You have to spend more time giving quality advice and not focusing just on product because the advice is really what distinguishes you and differentiates you from all these other models. It is also important that we figure out how to see more people, leveraging technology to make that happen. With things like Skype, we should be able to see 30 or 40 percent more people in a day. How can we use technology to help us find more people, develop stronger leads, and give more advice?

Life Insurance Challenges: It's Hard to Sell, and the Press Vilifies Advisors

I think there are a lot of reasons why our industry focuses on assets under management more than life insurance. There is no one reason. First of all, it is hard to sell life insurance. It is so much easier to sell a mutual fund or even an annuity. Selling life insurance is a complex process today, from how long that application is to all of the underwriting. It really is so hard. People often say, "Why bother?"

If an advisor has a relationship with a client on the investment side and then subjects the client to underwriting where he or she is declined, the advisor could be putting other business with that client at risk. So it is also easier for the advisor to say, "I'm just not going to do it."

But I believe there is another reason. In the press, people who sell life insurance are often vilified. They are certainly accused of not selling life insurance or annuities for the right reasons.

In the next decade, increasing and changing regulatory rules will be enacted that are going to make it increasingly difficult for people to give advice under a commission model. This will make it harder to get people motivated to want to sell life insurance. As a result, fewer Americans will get the help they need.

Throughout history, there have always been challenges. I think carriers and producers are highly creative, and so far we have always been able to adapt to all of the change. At the core, people need the products our industry offers. They need life insurance if they die too soon. They need disability insurance if they can't generate an income because they are disabled and out of work. They need savings for the future to be able to educate their children and to retire. And if all that isn't enough, we have this massive movement, the biggest movement of dollars in history, with people withdrawing and saying, "How do I guarantee an income?"

> For more than two hundred years, our industry has been helping protect American families' financial security. We will continue to because the need is much greater, but also because of the passion and commitment of those who work in the business.

I remain optimistic because I see some amazing creativity and innovate thinking across the industry. For more than two hundred years, our industry has been helping protect American families' financial security. We will continue to because the need is much greater, but also because of the passion and commitment of those who work in the business.

Life Insurance and Wise Planning Protect People's Futures

The Miracle of Life Insurance manifested itself in an unforgettable way in my agency back in 1975. The first person I ever hired as a producer did not come from the life insurance industry; he had previously sold cameras in retail. In his first two months on the job, he was at an agency in Norwalk, Connecticut, having coffee with the agency's life producer and one of the property and casualty producers. In the middle of the discussion, the P&C producer collapsed and died on the spot. The new agent, twenty-two years old or so, witnessed it. Later, the life producer told him about the financial planning he had done for the P&C producer to ensure that his wife and children would be well cared for. At that moment, this new producer understood the importance of the work he was doing.

CHAPTER 26

EILEEN C. MCDONNELL

Chairman and CEO

Penn Mutual

Philadelphia, Pennsylvania

Eileen has been chairman and chief executive officer of Penn Mutual since July 2013. She was appointed president in 2010 and CEO in 2011, after serving as chief marketing officer since 2008.

Before joining Penn Mutual, she was president of New England Financial, a wholly owned subsidiary of MetLife, and senior vice president of the Guardian Life Insurance Company. Eileen is a former member of the Master of Science in Management faculty at The American College in Bryn Mawr, Pennsylvania, where she held the newly endowed chair for Women and Financial Services. In 2015, The American College awarded Eileen the prestigious Solomon S. Huebner Gold Medal.

Eileen serves on the Board of Managers of Janney Montgomery Scott LLC, a wholly owned subsidiary of Penn Mutual. In 2013, she was named to the board of Universal Health Services, Inc. (NYSE: UHS). She is a member of the Audit Committee.

She is the author of *Marketing Financial Services to Women*.

A graduate of Molloy College in Rockville Centre, New York, Eileen majored in mathematics and computer science and received an honorary doctor of laws (LLD) degree in 2011. She earned her Master of Business Administration in finance and investments from Adelphi University in Garden City, New York, and was recognized in 2013 for outstanding service to the university.

EILEEN'S STORY

Life insurance has played a significant part in my life. It has allowed me to take time off from my career twice, accumulate cash value, and adopt my daughter, all with great confidence and financial security.

The One Advisor Who Asked Me the Most Important Question

I started in this industry in my early twenties by accident, as a lot of people do. I was a home office person and was around distribution people and advisors. I became the youngest vice president in Equitable history at age twenty-seven.

I was around agents all the time, but nobody ever asked me if I had a financial plan or any life insurance coverage because I was a single female.

I knew a woman advisor, Mary Lou Webber—now her last name is Salvati—and her father, Frank Queally. Mary Lou and her brother were both highly successful producers. One day, Mary Lou asked me, "Eileen, is anyone talking to you about your plan?"

I said, "To be honest with you, no." I was in all the agencies, in all those presentations, but nobody started that conversation with me, and I was not doing anything for myself. We sat down to talk and Mary Lou said, "I know you're single, but what are your plans?"

I had no immediate plans to be married. I had a big family, and I was close to my family. I was the doting aunt. Because I was successful, I was paying for my nephew's karate lessons and my nieces' ballet and gymnastics lessons that my sisters couldn't afford. I told Mary Lou that I would want those things to be able to continue if I weren't here. She said, "Let's get you insured with life insurance and see how much we can get. We will get you permanent life insurance. You don't know today necessarily what you might need it for, but you are healthier now than you will probably ever be, and you don't know where life is going to take you and when you are going to need this. It would be a great opportunity—not necessarily for the death benefit, but for retirement later on."

So off I went with that as a cornerstone in my plan— disability insurance and the other good things that round out a good financial plan— thanks to her asking me that question.

A Medical Diagnosis Hits Close to Home

In the fall of 2002, my dad was diagnosed with melanoma. At that time, I was running the individual business for Guardian as senior vice president. My father was considering hospice care, but he and my mom made the decision to keep him at home. He didn't want to be in a facility. I could throw money at the problem; I had the money to give them. I was one of six children, but my siblings had their own families and couldn't dedicate time to my dad's care. My parents needed my physical presence. My father was six feet tall and weighed 200 pounds, and my mother was petite. They also needed emotional support. I figured that at the end of the day, you can have many jobs, but you have only one father.

So I decided to step out of my role at Guardian because I wasn't able to dedicate myself the way I wanted to in my career and give what Guardian needed of me at the time. And I needed to feel comfortable that I was giving enough at home.

Fortunately for me, I was gone for only for four months. During that time, I got a call that MetLife would love for me to join them. Six months after I returned to MetLife, they named me president of New England Life Insurance Company.

Another Diagnosis—This Time, Mine

Now, fast-forward to just about the time I decided I was going to adopt my daughter in my early forties. I got diagnosed with melanoma as I was going through the process. My father had died a year and a half prior to that from melanoma, so of course my diagnosis fell really hard on me and my mother. Fortunately for me, it was in an early stage, and I had surgery and recovered. But at that point in time, I became uninsurable.

So I had the policy in place, and I had been building cash value since my twenties. I was able to have the death protection coverage in place that I needed, plus other financial planning that went along with that. Because I had life insurance, I could step out of a senior executive role. I was president of New England Financial when I decided to step out of corporate life to adopt my daughter, Claire. I took three years out of corporate life to be home with her, and that's when I was a professor at The American College. I taught an online course from home.

It was possible because of a plan that had started back in my twenties.

We Need to Take Single Professional Women Seriously

I would like to say the industry has gotten a lot better with taking single professional women seriously and helping them plan because you never know where the turns of life will take you. North Star and many other companies do it right. But when we look at the rates of women who are insured and underinsured, I think LIMRA still says women are insured at $0.60 on the dollar compared to their male counterparts, given the same demographics.

Life insurance gave me the privilege to make decisions a lot of people would love to make.

If I had not been in the business and approached by Mary Lou when I was young, I can't imagine where I would be now. Life insurance gave me the privilege to make decisions a lot of people would love to make. Having life insurance gives you a "permission slip" to do the things in life you need to do.

Advice to Advisors: Focus on Caring for People

No matter what generation you're in, there are always virtues among humans, and one of them is a deep, caring, affection and love for the people you hold dear. It may manifest itself differently for different people. If you go back just a couple of generations, my grandfather came from Ireland and emigrated here to have a better life and put food on the table. Then my dad worked hard to put us through good schools and get a good education. He wasn't present at all of our activities because of his commitment to his work, but that was his expression of love for his family. For today's dad, the expression of love might be driving through McDonald's for dinner and being at his kid's soccer game or basketball game.

But no matter how you slice it generationally, there will always be a need to care for, protect, and nurture those around you whom you hold dear, whether it is a family situation or a business situation.

My advice to advisors is to stay focused on that. There is a lot of distraction around financial engineering and the different bells and whistles on various products, but it all boils down to taking care of people.

> I ask every person I meet, "Are you thinking about the future? Are you planning for it?"

My belief in the business and the work we do spills into my daily life in terms of people I meet. I can't separate the two; this belief is embedded in my DNA. I ask every person I meet, "Are you thinking about the future? Are you planning for it?" Having gone through advocacy training, I know it is my obligation to have conversations with these folks who wouldn't ordinarily address the topic. I can't separate myself as a person thinking about career and personal life and vice versa.

There are things about my personal values that I bring to the workplace, and I don't think I could be in a job where I would have to separate the two.

Advice to Consumers: Buy Life Insurance Early in Your Life

From a consumer standpoint, this is a great business that allows people to fulfill their obligation to their families while protecting themselves and their hopes, dreams, and desires with one simple vehicle—permanent life insurance. Start early, and stay with it.

150

CHAPTER 27

GREGORY V. OSTERGREN

Chairman, President, and CEO

American National Property and Casualty Company

Springfield, Missouri

Greg joined American National Property and Casualty Company in 1990 as president and CEO. In 2000, he took on the additional role of chairman and led the acquisition of the Farm Family Insurance Group in 2001. Under his leadership, the company has enjoyed significant profitable growth and received several honors, including the Missouri Quality Award based on the Malcolm Baldrige criteria.

With more than thirty-nine years of experience in the insurance industry, Greg has become a recognized leader known for his skills and techniques as a high-level strategist. He has been a keynote speaker at numerous industry conferences and national seminars. He also is a board member of several industry associations.

Greg is a graduate of the University of Minnesota, with degrees in economics and mathematics. He began his insurance career in the actuarial area at Allstate Insurance Companies in Northbrook, Illinois. He and his wife, Diane, live in Springfield, Missouri. They have two children and six grandchildren.

GREG'S STORY

My Dad Was an Insurance Agent—A "First Economic Responder"

I am very fortunate because my father was a life insurance agent. Hearing so many of my dad's stories about the need for and the importance of insurance and those who offer it helped me realize that we are really the "first economic responders" who are there with a claim check when property is damaged or there is a liability or most importantly when an income earner dies.

As proud as I was of my dad's work and the importance of it, I didn't initially plan to join this industry. Because of my science and math background, I was looking at engineering as a career. There was a pretty severe recession at that time, however, and I saw several of my friends' fathers—who had great engineering jobs—get laid off. It opened me up to looking at other opportunities, and I saw the insurance industry as very well-managed and being essentially recession-proof. My father encouraged me to consider going into this business, and I saw that insurance would be a great career, even during a recession.

> It seems like people spend more time picking out new clothes than they do their insurance program, and I think that is a real disservice to them and especially to those who rely on them.

Advice to Consumers: Make Sure You Have Enough Coverage

My number one piece of advice to consumers is the same advice I give to friends and family: pay attention to your insurance coverage and its importance to your family's or business's future—not just life insurance but all types of insurance coverage. I find that most people actually do not have a good insurance program. It seems like people spend more time picking out new clothes than they do their insurance program, and I think that is a real disservice to them and especially to those who rely on them.

I'd also caution people against working solely with direct distributions and "call for a quote" companies. I just don't think that experience ultimately compares well to working with an advisor who knows the importance of

152

having the right insurance program—someone who can sit down with you, get to know your needs, and design a plan specifically for your unique situation.

The most expensive insurance program you can have is one that really doesn't serve your needs.

Advice to Agents and Advisors: Make Life Insurance the Foundation of Every Financial Plan

In my father's day, financial advisors were proudly referred to as "insurance salesmen," which was actually considered a pretty noble title and profession. Many of my age will remember the popular television show *Father Knows Best*, in which the father was a life insurance salesman and exemplary member of the community. I think at times we may have strayed too far from that concept and lost sight of the foundational importance of life insurance.

This shift really began in the 1980s. During that era, a lot of people ceased becoming insurance agents and became financial advisors, abandoning the middle market in droves. We saw many companies and agents adopt the mantra "buy term, invest the difference." Interest rates were extremely high, and it was a fairly easy sale. The great products like whole life became relics of the past. Of course it fell down because the vast majority of those policies never paid off anything. And, worst of all, people didn't *invest* the difference; they *blew* the difference. So what did they end up with? I believe as an industry, we let people down with this approach.

We all know that a proper plan maximizes the probability of a client's financial success. We do that through appropriate investment contributions, diversifications of investments, etc. I am in no way saying that the role of a skilled financial advisor isn't vital, but even the best financial plan can fall apart instantly if the husband, wife, or business partner dies.

In my opinion, the only way to truly diversify that risk and have a higher probability of success is through life insurance. It's very much the foundation of any financial plan.

Some advisors may hesitate to start here because it can certainly be uncomfortable talking about mortality with a client. But you can discuss this in terms of diversification and the importance of maximizing your probability of success rather than talking about the negatives of somebody dying.

Let's Bring Our Industry into the Twenty-First Century

Let's face it, our industry is rather archaic in what we do today. The processes tend to take forever. We use relic language—terms that confuse and frustrate people. I think that in many respects, the industry itself has caused a decrease in the focus on life insurance.

Let's face it, our industry is rather archaic in what we do today. The processes tend to take forever. We use relic language— terms that confuse and frustrate people.

I think of mail order as a comparison. Back in the 1970s and '80s, you would order something from a catalog, and it would take six to eight weeks for delivery. Today you can have a wonderful shopping experience and get your order delivered the next day, in many cases.

The life insurance industry is like the old catalog business. Ironically though, the products have never been better or more affordable. It is absolutely incredible what the industry offers today that is available versus any other time in history, yet we don't have the take-up. It's time to bring our business into the twenty-first century!

So how do we drag ourselves into the modern era? I think it's by focusing on a powerfully simple experience that makes sure our clients are satisfied, not frustrated with us.

A company we recently partnered with to help drive our innovation efforts did a survey about people's emotional perceptions of the insurance industry. When many people first hear about insurance, the first thing that comes to their minds is frustration. Number two is confusion, number three is anxiety, and four is boredom. Insurance should instead give people confidence, relief, and satisfaction. But we've got a long way to go. It's incumbent upon all of us in the insurance industry to turn that around and do a much better job. Other industries are becoming a lot easier to work with and understand, and they take a lot of the frustration and confusion out of the process. The insurance industry is lagging in that area. And we have to do the same thing for our field forces. We are too difficult for our field forces to work with as well. As I regularly remind my team, people—both consumers and agents—will only put up with us as an industry until something better and easier comes along. Something better and easier always comes along.

> **The products that companies offer today are the best that have ever been designed and are the most affordable they've ever been.**

We Have Reason to Be Optimistic

Despite our challenges, I'm very optimistic about the future of this industry because the need for insurance is greater than ever and the importance of what we do hasn't shrunk a bit. The products that companies offer today are the best that have ever been designed and are the most affordable they've ever been.

There's also an increasing focus on improving the experience and reducing frustration. I see a lot of insurance companies now that are working on this very concept of making insurance a lot easier to apply for and understand. I think there is a lot of hope for the future in our industry.

Consumer preferences are also moving favorably in our direction, thanks to a couple of major events. First, a lot of the universal life insurance policies sold in the '80s were sold at very high interest rates. As time went on, people became confused and frustrated when they had to put in a lot more money than what they had planned just to keep their policy in force. As a result, a lot of policies lapsed, leaving a bad taste in consumers' mouths. Today, however, interest rates are extremely low, and policies being sold should hold up very well. Second, during the 2008 financial meltdown, people saw their investments fluctuate quite a bit, which caused a lot of anxiety. Yet insurance policies came out very strong. Also, as a concept, "investing the difference" is not nearly as attractive today.

With these lessons still fresh, I see people going back to really understanding the value of some of the older products like whole life. I think there is a growing receptivity among consumers of the importance and value of our products through changing economic times. I think there's a tremendous opportunity to step up, take advantage of that, and help people be better protected.

Personal Experiences Underscore the Importance of What We Do

I talked earlier about my exposure to the importance of life insurance, thanks to my dad's career. It's a lesson that has been reinforced throughout my life through some tough personal experiences.

My son-in-law passed away tragically from a brain tumor, and that was, of course, very hard. Fortunately, he had life insurance; unfortunately, it wasn't enough for our daughter and her three small children. I look back and see that because I am in the insurance business, it was my responsibility to at least have some of the discussions about how much he should have secured. We did have discussions on the importance of life insurance, and he ended up purchasing some life insurance outside of his work in addition to what his company provided, but the combination still wasn't adequate.

A call from my older sister also drove home the importance of a good life insurance plan. She spent thirty years working for an outstanding company. The company is regularly recognized among the top one hundred companies worldwide to work for. In fact, she always bragged about all the benefits. Long story short, she called me about six months after she retired. Her husband had been diagnosed with leukemia. They had bought their life insurance through her company, which is very proud of its superb benefits, only to find out that after you retire, coverage drops considerably. She said, "Now I need it the most, and it won't be there." I'll never forget how helpless I felt in that moment and how recommitted I became to the mission of insurance.

These personal experiences translate back to my advice for consumers and financial advisors alike: really understand what you have so that you can make sure it is there when you might need it most. Things do change, especially today.

CHAPTER 28

MONTRI SAENG-URAIPORN

President

Proactive Training & Consultant Co., Ltd.

Bangrak, Bangkok, Thailand

Since 2010, Montri has been the president of Proactive Training and Consultant, a professional training and coaching firm.

For almost twenty-three years, he was a Senior Agency Consultant and Senior District Manager for American International Assurance Co. Ltd .in the Bangkok metropolitan area. He joined the company as a life insurance agent and moved through the ranks to be a supervisor, unit manager, and district manager. He was selected to be among the first group of AIA Ambassadors. After that, Montri was the Chief Agency Officer of Ace Life Assurance Thailand for thirty-two months and president of Finansa Life Assurance in Thailand for three years.

Previously, Montri served as Advertising Sales Manager of *Business Review* magazine and *Who Is Who* magazine.

During Montri's term as president of the Thai Association of Life Insurance and Financial Advisors from 1999 to 2003, the membership grew from a few hundred to more than ten thousand. And the association's financial strength grew from less than 30,000 baht to more than 22 million baht, which allowed the association to acquire its own building, fully decorated, with zero debt in 2002.

Montri holds a master's degree in business administration and management from Chulalongkorn University, a bachelor's degree in political science from Ramkhamhaeng University, and a certificate in business/commerce from Assumption Commercial College.

MONTRI'S STORY

Two Questions from My Brother Brought Me into the Business

I was born and raised in Bangkok, Thailand. After I graduated from Assumption Commercial College, a Catholic school, at the age of twenty, I worked as a salesman in various jobs. My love affair with life insurance began in 1981 at the age of twenty-six. My elder brother, Chooluck, had been working in the life insurance business for two years and was building his own team. He asked me to go to his house, so I did. He asked me two simple questions. The first one was, "How is your job as an advertising sales manager for a monthly English-language business publication? Is it difficult to sell advertising?"

My answer was, "I think it is difficult for a majority of people, but not for me. I see many who have failed, but I know that in selling anything, if you see enough people, you can succeed."

Then he asked me another question: "If there were a sales job that is equally difficult but you could earn three to five times more, would you be interested?"

My answer was yes, and after learning more about the career, I started working as a full-time life insurance agent with him at American International Assurance Company in October 1981. By 1982, I had become one of the top five agents nationally.

How Norman Levine Helped Change the Industry Globally

The person who impacted me the most and inspired me to dedicate my career to the industry is Norman G. Levine (1926–2015). In his closing speech of the First Asia Pacific Life Insurance Congress (APLIC) in Singapore in 1991, Norman Levine told us about the evolution of the life insurance agency system in the United States—how it moved from a career that many people looked down on to be a career in which many agents and advisors gained respect from their clientele and from the public. That shift happened because some industry leaders not only worked hard to become successful and served as role models; they also worked on upgrading the industry, shared what they knew, and helped build organizations that educate people in the industry and raise their level of esteem.

> Thanks to all those legends, the industry became more effective at serving the public, and the perception of the industry improved.

Mr. Levine commended Vincent Chua, the founding president of the Singapore Life Underwriters Association, who spent ten years establishing and formalizing the Life Underwriters Association in Singapore. He challenged everyone in the audience to go back to their respective countries to do something. I was there, and I took it as a challenge to go back to my country (Thailand) and start doing something. By then, I was the president of LICA (the Life Insurance Counselors Association), an in-house association of AIA. As a committee, we decided to do more than the traditional functions of just organizing monthly meetings; we started hosting seminars in various regions of the country and organizing an annual seminar to raise funds for charity. We later set up a foundation to give scholarships to poor students.

In 1998, we reactivated the Thai Life Underwriters Association, brought in speakers to share best practices, began publishing *Insurance Magazine*, bid for and organized the 6th APLIC (Asia Pacific Life Insurance Congress) in Bangkok in 2001, brought in and moderated an LUTC (Life Underwriter Training Council) class to help thousands of agents do their jobs better, and, with kind support from Phillip C. Richards, formed GAMA Thailand in 2004. In 2010, we hosted another APLIC meeting in Bangkok.

Thanks to the inspiration of the role models and mentors I mentioned, I chose to start my consultancy work in 2010. I had two primary goals. First, I aimed to help leaders in Thailand have systems to build their organizations. Second, I aimed to help advisors have systems to build their customer-centric careers and to build their futures by helping their prospects and clients have clarity of what they want and a clear plan to achieve it.

Advice for Consumers: Have a Clear Life Goal, Start Preparing Early, and Protect Your Future Income with Life Insurance

My advice for today's customer/client is that in this time of change, the solution is to have clarity. The best way to avoid confusion and live a good life in a changing environment, as we are in today, is to have clarity about what you really want out of life. Financial planning is a necessary component of life planning. Look for a financial advisor who can help you achieve that clarity and then provide you with a plan to achieve your life goals.

Start preparing for your future early in your life. The earlier you start, the better; you will have more time to accumulate wealth to achieve your goal, and you will have more time to reap the happiness after you have achieved it.

> Your most important financial asset is not your house, your equity account, or your business. Your most important financial asset is your future income.

Finally, realize that your most important financial asset is not your house, your equity account, or your business. Your most important financial asset is your future income. With the steady flow of future income and with the potential growth in assets that comes as years go by, you can achieve most everything you want in life. So while you focus on building your wealth by trying to find ways to increase your yield and ROI (return on investment), don't forget the most important asset—your future income. Make sure that you protect your future income by having enough life insurance as the basis of your financial plan. With your future income, you can take care of yourself and your family and build financial independence. Life insurance is a critical part of that financial independence for your family.

My Advice to Advisors: Work for Independence, Practice Delayed Gratification, and Work for Work

My advice to advisors is to set your goal, and have your end in mind to achieve independence. Real success in life is to have independence, both in terms of time and finances to live the life you want with the ones you love. When you set your goal to achieve independence, you will have to work hard and focus on practicing delayed gratification, both in building your business and building your savings and investment portfolio. In business, you will learn to think big, start small, and build deep to build a strong clientele that will provide you not only high income in the present but also long-term income that will come from recurring sales and referrals. In terms of your finances, delayed gratification will help you save more and have more funds to invest so that you can attain your financial goals.

> When you set your goal to achieve independence, you will have to work hard and focus on practicing delayed gratification, both in building your business and building your savings and investment portfolio.

In building your business, your income comes from people you deal with in your everyday work. I would like to suggest that when you are with people, when you work with your prospects or clients, forget yourself and focus on them. When you take facts, focus on them. When you plan for and make recommendations, focus on them. Working for money or fame can bring you success, but working for work and for the people you serve will get you everything. It is like the analogy of chasing a butterfly. If you want to catch a butterfly and try to chase it, it will fly away, and even in the end, when you catch it, you might not be satisfied with that one; you want more. If you want the butterfly, don't chase it; focus on developing yourself and on making yourself attractive. It will voluntary come to you— not just one, but many. When you try to understand what your clients want and work on improving yourself, you will be more useful and create more value to them.

Unfortunately, the "Aware" Sale Is Easier than the "Unaware" Sale

I think the reason our industry has moved away from focusing on life insurance is quite obvious: given a choice, most people will look for an easier way to do things. Unfortunately, the method that provides an easy short-term benefit can potentially bring unfavorable results in the long term.

Since the emergence of the universal life and investment-linked products, and our industry's move from just life insurance to diversification, life insurance agents and financial advisors have a choice to focus on selling the *essence* or the *easy*, and the one many choose is obvious. Many of agency leaders also take to the easier part in training and developing their advisors.

As the great Norman Levine used to say, "There are three sales in our industry: the easy sell, the aware sell, and the unaware sell."

The easy, or aware, sell is selling greed and yield.

Most people are aware that they need general insurance, but most people are unaware that they need life insurance. The "unaware" sale is more difficult. That is why advisors need to have people skills in addition to product-knowledge and presentation skills. They need to be able to sell themselves, sell trust, help prospects find out what they want, and help them make the right decisions. They don't need all of that to do the easy, or "aware" sale. Moving away from life insurance as the main focus will cause the agency system to slowly lose its main essence—the system by which trusted advisors work with and serve the public. Trusted advisors help people clarify what they want and provide them with practical plans and review to achieve those goals, even during the uncontrollable events of life, whether it's dying too soon, living too long, or dodging hazards along the way. The easy sale (investment yield) and the aware sale (general insurance, health insurance, and disability insurance) will help solve the problems of living too long and dodging hazards along the way.

But life insurance is the only product that will solve the dying too soon part.

People die every day. When that happens without life insurance in place, there are great losses of earning power in that person's family. Without adequate life insurance, nothing flows back into the system.

How We Help People Create Tomorrow Today Through Life Insurance

In 1982, I attended a seminar for agents and managers from Malaysia, Brunei, Singapore, Philippines, and Thailand. The theme was ""Create Tomorrow…Today," and the keynote speaker was Mr. Gamini S. Korala, the most respected and most productive senior manager of AIA in the entire region for many years. He impressed on everyone in the audience, including me, that we had the opportunity to build our own futures and that every day, we are creating tomorrow by doing what we do today. It's not important who you were in the past; what is important is what you want to be and what you do every day to make it happen. I also learned that as a product, life insurance is the only way that people can create tomorrow today for their family members and their loved ones. Life insurance is the only way a person can guarantee future income for their loved ones.

> Life insurance is the only way that people can create tomorrow today for their family members and their loved ones.

During that seminar, Gamini told us how his love story with the business began. He was a Sri Lankan who immigrated to Singapore during World War II. After the war, he continued to work in Singapore as a clerk and sold life insurance part time to earn extra income. One of his friends, who became one of his first clients, was a famous sportsman who eventually bought from Gamini because he believed that "A good man will always bring good things." He told Gamini, "You are a good man, so I will follow your recommendation." A year later, that client was diagnosed with cancer and battled it for a long time. Before he passed away, he asked to meet with Gamini and told him, "I have many friends, but not one of them can help me. The only friend I can trust to take care of my family is you. Can you promise me that my family will be okay?"

Gamini said he gave his word. After the funeral, he learned that none of the installments on the house or furniture had been paid since his client had become ill; his client's wife did not work outside the home. The widow cried and said she didn't know what would happen next. Gamini told her, "Do not worry. Your husband did something that will take care of it." Gamini processed the claim and went back to that house again several days later. He said he saw several people standing in front of the house. He hid behind a tree near the house to see what happened. He heard his friend's son cry out, "Mama is not home. You'd better leave!" Evidently, the men were there to seize some assets the family had been unable to pay for.

> While most salespeople are going to the widow's home to take something back, we are going to the door to deliver a check to the widow and her family.

After the people left, Gamini walked to the house. When the boy saw him, he excitedly ran into the house calling, "Mommy, the insurance uncle is here!" Gamini told us that on that day, he felt he was greater than all the other salesmen. While most salespeople are going to the widow's home to take something back, we are going to the door to deliver a check to the widow and her family.

Gamini gave his friend's widow the claim check. He advised her to use part of the money to pay off all the debt, to save some of it as an education fund for the children, and to use part of the fund to redecorate the house to be a day-care center so that she could have an income to take care of herself and the children.

From then on, Gamini said he devoted his life to the life insurance business. That situation changed Gamini's life, and it impacted the lives of the people in the audience that day, including me. I am fortunate that I don't have to wait for the same kind of experience to happen to me before I believe in the product and the profession. I was quite young when I entered the business, and it took many years before I witnessed the same kind of experience myself.

The learning experience from the "Create Tomorrow…Today" seminar in 1982 helped me realize the basic fact of life: we all can create our tomorrow by doing what we do today. It helped me understand and appreciate the product we sell. It is the only product in the world that can help people create and secure their tomorrow today. Ours is the only profession that helps people be clear about what they want to happen in the future and to make sure that it will happen with the Miracle of Life Insurance.

The Regulatory Environment in Thailand

Today, the regulatory environment in Thailand is friendly, and people are working together. To promote the business and to protect consumers, our regulators work with companies to open multiple channels of distribution.

To educate the public and the advisors, the regulators work with the agent association to provide continuing-education classes to help our agents become trusted financial advisors.

The structure of the insurance business in Thailand followed the business formation in the United States. In 1968, our government established the Office of Insurance, which later became the Department of Insurance under the Ministry of Commerce. In 1968, the insurance companies were encouraged to form trade associations. The Life Underwriters Association was formed at that time.

GAMA Thailand (the General Agents and Managers Association) was established in 2004 and began to be well known and well accepted by many leaders in the industry.

In 2007, to prepare to enter the Asian Economic Committee (AEC) and to open the market for the investment-linked and more diversified products, the government changed the structure of the regulation body to be independent committee under the Ministry of Finance. This new body is empowered by the government to regulate insurance companies, brokers, and agents under the name of the Office of Insurance Commission (OIC). Its role is to supervise insurance-business conduct. The government also encouraged the formation of National Association of Insurance Business, which comprises committee from all major associations in the insurance business—namely, the Thai General Insurance Association, Thai Life Insurance Association, Thai Brokers Association, Thai Association of Insurance and Financial Advisors (TAIFA), and Thailand Society of Actuaries.

> In the past decade, our regulators have worked with life insurance companies to open new channels of distribution, from using agency system as the only channel of distribution to multiple channels comprised of agency, bank, telemarketing, direct marketing, and broker units.

I think the main focus of all regulators is the same: to promote the business to the public and to protect consumers. In the past decade, our regulators have worked with life insurance companies to open new channels of distribution, from using agency system as the only channel of distribution to multiple channels comprised of agency, bank, telemarketing, direct marketing, and broker units. The strategy has worked quite well. Annual new life insurance sales in Thailand improved from 1.4 million policies in 2004 to 3.2 million policies in 2014, a 129 percent increase. The policies in force grew from 7.8 million policies in 2004 to 19.4 million policies in 2014, a 149 percent increase. The majority of this growth came from non-agency channels.

Regulators also worked with the companies and TAIFA to promote the life insurance business to the public through community education programs. They also jointly organize Annual National Life Insurance Day to promote the benefit of life insurance to the public.

The regulators also started requiring proof of continued-education hours as part of the requirements to renew agent licenses and investment licenses to sell investment products. The continued-education program is organized by the regulators, an educational institute, and TAIFA. These credit requirements and the new trend of selling more diversified products has reduced the number of agents. But sales through the agency channel moderately increased, and many companies have turned their focus to building more professional agents with higher per capita production and make Million Dollar Round Table eligibility as the benchmark for the standard of excellence. This new trend also helps foster the relationships among TAIFA, the companies, and the regulators. TAIFA provides a platform to promote MDRT, as well as sessions and educational programs to raise the esteem of the profession and the individual agents who achieve MDRT status.

As a result of these developments, I think the future of life insurance sales in Thailand looks bright. There is a new mind-set of quality, with more education and training being devoted to the business on the agency side and a new focus on improving agency management's ability to attract, select, build, and grow the right people.

Witnessing the significant turnarounds in the industry in the USA, in Singapore, and later in Thailand provides me with strong hope and a belief that the future of our industry will be stronger and can continue to be more and more useful to the public in each respective country. We have great people in the industry who are working hard— not only for their own good but to improve the standard of best practices. They care, they share, they grow, and they help their peers and the younger generations to grow in the process. Together, we can bring back the religion of life insurance.

> **Together, we can bring back the religion of life insurance.**

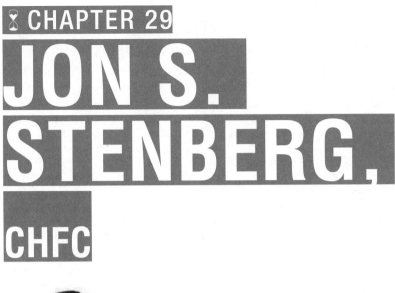

CHAPTER 29

JON S. STENBERG, CHFC

Executive Vice President and
General Manager – Insurance

RiverSource Life Insurance Company/
Ameriprise Financial

Minneapolis, Minnesota

Jon S. Stenberg is Executive Vice President and General Manager – Insurance for RiverSource Life Insurance Company/Ameriprise Financial in Minneapolis, Minnesota. He is a member of the Board of Trustees for The American College and of the Board of Directors of Secure Retirement Institute for LIMRA/LOMA.

Before assuming his current role, Jon served as Senior Vice President of the Individual Life Department of New York Life Insurance Co. He was responsible for overseeing the Retail Insurance division of the Individual Life Department. He also oversaw the UBS Insurance Agency at UBS Financial, including all key operations of product development, systems, and distribution. Previously, Jon served as Vice President of Life Insurance Sales of Lincoln Financial. He also worked at Aetna Life and served in the US Army.

After earning a bachelor of science degree in business administration from Central Michigan University, Jon went on to complete his Master of Business Administration at The Wharton School of the University of Pennsylvania.

JON'S STORY

From Fascination with the Product to Appreciation of Its Impact

My love affair with life insurance started with my first job out of college; I realized that it was a wonderfully complex product. I just loved all the different moving parts and how many different designs and purposes it had. I realized that it could be almost anything to anybody, depending on how you structured it, sold it, and designed it and designed the case. That complexity just fascinated me.

When I moved from behind the scenes in a finance-product role to the front lines to work as a wholesaler, the meaning of life insurance changed for me. It moved from being a complex model in a computer with complex reserving, statutory accounting, and gap accounting to a valuable product that helped people. I saw the people first and the product second, and then I saw what we were trying to accomplish in these sales. It was wonderful—I got to go home at the end of the day knowing I had I helped keep a business in the family so the family didn't have to break it up to pay taxes, for example. With the policies I have placed over time, I know that there will be families who did not have to move out of their houses and move into Section 8 housing, and the kids can go to the colleges they want to attend.

> **Families who have life insurance don't have to deal with a financial tragedy in the middle of having to deal with an emotional tragedy.**

I woke up to and became really impassioned around life insurance when it moved from being a really cool, complex model to "Holy moly, when I get to the end of my career, I know for a fact that because of the hard work I did, there will be businesses that stayed in the family and families who stayed together because of life insurance." Life insurance can help survivors avoid the squabbling that can too often cause years of resentment among survivors. They will feel that they have been treated fairly. And families who have life insurance don't have to deal with a financial tragedy in the middle of having to deal with an emotional tragedy.

We Need to Address Demographic and Cultural Shifts

I think our industry is challenged in growth today because there are a couple of headwinds.

One is a demographic headwind. Generations are further apart than they used to be, and that will have an impact on sales. There are fewer kids than there used to be per family, and that will have an impact on sales. Plus, some younger people today are not self-reliant like we were when I was growing up.

I grew up in the era when I had two or three jobs in middle school and two or three jobs in high school. I joined the army, paid for my own college, worked two or three jobs during college, and then paid off my own student loans and bought my own car. If you make a kid do that today, he will almost call child protective services on you.

So today there is this sense that I don't need life insurance, even if I am twenty-eight with a kid, because the reality is that Mom and Dad will help pay for everything because the moms and dads of today *are* generationally wealthier than the moms and dads used to be when I grew up. Depending on Mom and Dad is a really bad plan, as we know. That is the mind-set of certainly some Millennials, and guess what? From a policy-count standpoint, people who are twenty-five to thirty-five are prime buyers of small term insurance policies, and we are struggling there.

The second headwind is that there has been a cultural shift. Our industry has not cracked the code on how to gain excitement among some of the emerging demographics like the LGBT community, African Americans, and Hispanics. We have not done a very good job of getting them to embrace life insurance, in my opinion, and they are becoming a larger percentage of our population.

As our population becomes less white, we have to adapt to the demographics.

Some companies are working really hard on that, and it is a challenging issue. There is no easy solution here, and it is something we are going to have to continue to work really hard at.

Let's Hire More Young People to Provide Life Insurance

In addition, our industry has moved away from hiring young people, so there are fewer mouths talking about the Miracle of Life Insurance. That will directly result in fewer purchases, so that is a challenge. The Internet has not replaced the thousands and thousands of people we would hire and train as an industry whom we don't hire and train now. Some companies are doing that, but if you look at the numbers, as an agent force, our agents are getting older and older. That is a challenge also.

The Miracle of Life Insurance is still there, and it is more important than ever because taxes are only going up. People need to be thoughtful and plan for their future, and life insurance is a critical part of that. This is important whether it is protecting one spouse from another spouse's income loss so that first spouse can retire in the way he or she wants or protecting the family from what I believe will be increasing income and estate taxes in the future. Life insurance is an important solution in both cases.

Advice to Clients: Life Insurance Is More Affordable than Ever, So Buy a Lot of It

What was needed twenty years ago is still needed today—the financial-planning formula for middle America and that age group from twenty-five or thirty up to forty-five or fifty. The formula that existed in the '80s and '90s is a great formula. Each company may have a slightly different take on this, but my formula is to both protect your income and build tax-advantaged savings.

You protect your income through disability insurance and term insurance, and you build your tax-protected savings in a permanent cash value life insurance policy that is heavily funded. Now, the cool thing about the formula is that it is much cheaper today than it was in the 1980s. If you just label a chart "cost of coverage" and "insurance ownership in America," you may come to the conclusion that all we have to do is *increase* prices, and we'll sell more. So clients can take advantage of the Miracle of Life Insurance at a cost that is significantly discounted from the cost their parents would have had to pay.

> It is more affordable than ever, so it is a little bit nutty that our fellow Americans are not protecting themselves now that prices have come down.

When insurance salesmen went door to door or factory to factory back in the 1930s and '40s and collected those premiums, it was a huge burden on families; it was a huge chunk of their income. But they knew it was important. Now the premium is a small fraction of somebody's substantial income for protecting their families' future, yet we're doing it at a lower percentage than ever before. It is a little bit baffling, but it is good news for those who wake up—the solution is more affordable than ever.

> You can't get people to secure life insurance based on logic—you need to hit them in the heart.

It is just crazy that people would put their families at risk by failing to buy something that is so affordable. And if they don't want to buy the whole life policy, the passionate part of me that wants to protect those kids wants to see them at least get term insurance until the kids get to college.

> Don't make those kids suffer later because you want to buy them an Xbox today.

Here at Ameriprise, we compiled a book featuring Ameriprise clients whose lives and families were dramatically impacted by the Miracle of Life Insurance and also disability income. You can't get people to secure life insurance based on logic—you need to hit them in the heart.

A Note from the Authors

Here at North Star Resource Group, we took a historical look back at the cost of insurance over the past half century. Our premise was that the actual cost of insurance to provide the same amount of coverage was going down. We based our research on using the same client profile of a forty-five-year-old male, preferred nonsmoking, purchasing a whole life insurance policy (life-to-100). We started in the year 1965 and did the last calculation in 2013. The cost of insurance today is 22 percent of what it was in terms of premium paid as a percentage of the face amount.

How many other products in the marketplace today cost one-fifth of what they did half a century ago? It's simply remarkable, yet much of the public is unaware of such pricing advantages they have today with insurance products. This is demonstrated by the research conducted for the LIMRA *Insurance Barometer Study*, 2016.

Estimated Cost of Term Insurance

While many have put off buying life insurance because they believe it costs too much, consumers tend to overestimate the price. For instance, when asked how much a $250,000 term life policy would be for a healthy thirty-year-old, the median estimate was $400 more than twice the actual cost (see chart below).

The median estimate for consumers under thirty (who would typically pay less for coverage) was $500. And overall, nearly half of consumers believe the cost would be at least $500 annually, while one in four think it would cost at least $1,000 per year.

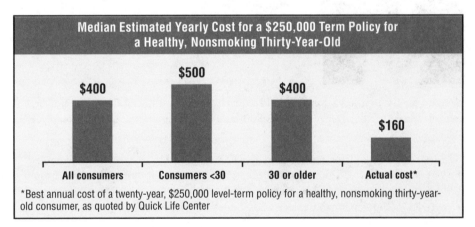

Median Estimated Yearly Cost for a $250,000 Term Policy for a Healthy, Nonsmoking Thirty-Year-Old

All consumers	Consumers <30	30 or older	Actual cost*
$400	$500	$400	$160

*Best annual cost of a twenty-year, $250,000 level-term policy for a healthy, nonsmoking thirty-year-old consumer, as quoted by Quick Life Center

Data and explanation provided by 2016 *Insurance Barometer Study*, Life Happens and LIMRA. Keep in mind that each individual's situation may vary.

As one can see, insurance costs have gone down considerably over the past fifty years, yet the average consumer is unaware of the reduction in the price of life insurance.

Advisors hold the key to educating the public about this favorable pricing of life insurance today. Our hope is that more people become educated through knowledgeable advisors who understand the importance of risk management in a client's overall planning strategy.

CHAPTER 30

MAURICE STEWART,

CLU, CHFC, CLF

Business Leader, Author, Speaker

Executive Consultant for Penn Mutual

Philadelphia, Pennsylvania

Growing up in rural Iowa during World War II, Maury lost his mother at an early age and was forced to take over his family's 800-acre farm when he was only fourteen years old.

In 1948, Maury enlisted in the Army Air Force and just three years later, he joined the war effort in Korea. Taking great pride in defending his country's freedom, Maury flew more than fifty bombing missions. Because of his courageous efforts, Maury was recognized in The American College's 2009 book *The American College Salutes The Greatest Generation*.

He married in 1952 and started his career as an agent for Penn Mutual in its Topeka, Kansas, location. Maury took over the company's Philadelphia office in 1960, and it became the top agency for Penn Mutual for twelve consecutive years under his leadership. Maury has dedicated his life and career to touching the lives of thousands of people through delivering what he calls the Miracle of Life Insurance.

In addition to his long-lasting commitment with Penn Mutual, Maury has made many contributions to The American College, particularly to the Chartered Leadership

Fellow® program. He has worked since the beginning concept stages by generously providing his knowledge and expertise on leadership. The CLF® program delivers four capstones every year, and from 1999 to 2004, Maury taught in all of them. He believes that because of the relevant coursework and skills training, The American College is the fundamental source of education in our industry.

Maury strongly believes in giving back to the community and to the industry that has been so good to him. He is President of the Board of the Visiting Nurse Association of Greater Philadelphia, where he actively strives to make a difference in people's lives. He has been a member of GAMA International since 1955. In 2004, Maury was recognized with the honor of induction into GAMA's Hall of Fame, which he feels is one of his greatest achievements.

Through the joint effort of The Penn Mutual Life Insurance Company and The American College, the recently endowed Maurice L. Stewart Lectureship honors Maury as one of its most esteemed and accomplished colleagues.

The series honors the lifelong contributions Maury has made not only to Penn Mutual, but also to The American College and the entire life insurance industry. The lectures help ensure that future generations of life insurance professionals know of Maury's outstanding career, his dedication to others, and his pursuit of excellence in leadership.

The annual lecture features top thought leaders from diverse disciplines who address themes and issues critical to the practice of leadership development. Maury is closely involved in the selection of speakers, ensuring that new ideas are featured at each lecture. The first lectureship took place in the fall of 2009. It was open to the industry and webcast across the country, as are all of the lectures.

Also in 2009, Maury was inducted into The American College Hall of Fame.

MAURY'S STORY

A Passion for the Miracle of Life Insurance

In 2013, Maury collaborated with GAMA International and published a book filled with fascinating and informative stories and his wisdom. It's titled *The Miracle Business: A Lifetime of Lessons on Leadership*.

In the book, he describes why he is passionate about life insurance and how he came to be known for using the phrase "the Miracle of Life Insurance":

> My passion is life insurance. I truly believe it provides miracles to people just when they need them most. These same miracles exist across the insurance and financial services industry—from those who provide financial protection against loss to those who help people achieve their dreams of retirement. We who have made this our career serve a noble purpose. We have an emotional attachment to the work we do for our clients and for the agents and advisors we recruit and develop. We commit to those we serve just as new doctors take the Hippocratic Oath to practice medicine ethically and honestly and to serve others those who enter the clergy take vows to guide and serve others spiritually.

> My passion is life insurance. I truly believe it provides miracles to people just when they need them most.

> Years ago, I attended an address by Dr. Solomon Huebner, the "father of insurance education," in which he described "the Miracle of Life Insurance" as a sound financial product that would provide security for people's families and businesses.

> I have used that phrase my entire career in discussing financial planning with clients, in teaching new associates about the need for life insurance, and in speeches I have given to companies and industry organizations.

> Some might think I am using a little hyperbole. But if it was good enough for Dr. Huebner, who in 1927 wrote a groundbreaking book about our business called *The Economics of Life Insurance*, then it's good enough for me. I truly believe that life insurance is the foundation for any solid financial planning.[8]

How a Colonel's Death Set My Career Path in Motion

When I came back from Korea, they wouldn't let me fly much, so they put me in charge of what they called the Personal Affairs Office, which took care of all the benefits for all the air force people. We had a large supply group that supplied the US Air Force. When we had a death, my job was to work with the priest, rabbi, or minister to administer the benefits the government would provide and any other benefits that the family might have.

---

8. Maurice L. Stewart, The Miracle Business: A Lifetime of Lessons on Leadership (Falls Church, Virginia: GAMA International, 2013), 1.

We were phasing in what we called the B47, which was the first hot jet bomber we had. They wouldn't let us junior guys fly too much. The senior guys were the main pilots because it was a hot airplane that they gave most of the hours to. I knew several of the senior guys, and the thing that really got me started was that we had a colonel who was probably one of the best pilots I had ever seen, ever flown with. The B47 was a great airplane except that it was a big kerosene can that had very little flight time. They hadn't really tested it adequately. The colonel blew. The plane crashed, and all three men in the crew were killed. They were all senior officers, so most of them were married and had families. The chaplain and I started working with the colonel's widow, Mary.

The most tragic part was when we found out that as they had blown, we had gone out to the house and Mary was just coming back from Chicago with her five kids. Her family was in Chicago, and they had been visiting. The neighbors told us that they were coming back on the five-something train. So we went down and met Mary and the five kids. I took Mary off to the side, and the chaplain took the kids off. I had to tell Mary about her husband's death. Over a period of time in working with her, we realized that the government benefits really weren't that much. They had a $20,000 USGLI—I think that's what we called it—and $10,000 of term life insurance. As we worked with her, one of the last times we spent with her, we were trying to work out all the details, saying the prayers, and doing all the things you possibly can. Then all at once, she totally broke down. She had really been a real trooper up until that point. I said, "Mary, what can we do?"

> I had to tell Mary about her husband's death. Over a period of time in working with her, we realized that the government benefits really weren't that much.

She said, "You can't do anything. I just realized that I have to go back to work. I can afford to keep only two of the kids. I have two cousins and an aunt who are each taking one of the other kids. So I'm breaking up the family." She and her husband had been so proud of their family.

The chaplain and I left. On the drive back to Topeka, we stopped at a little roadside place. He asked me, "What are you going to do when you get out of the air force?"

I said, "Well, I know I'm going to sell something. I don't want to be in the bureaucracy."

He said, "You're going to sell life insurance, aren't you?"

"Where did you get that?" I asked.

He said, "Let me ask you a question. If you had walked in there tonight with $100,000, do you think that Mary would have kept those kids together as a family?"

Now, $100,000 was a lot of money in 1952. I said, "Yes."

"Case closed," the chaplain told me. "Take a look into the business."

Marilyn, my wonderful wife, had moved to Topeka, and we had gotten married.

Ironically, she was working for the governor of Kansas. Paul Jernigan, who was the General Agent for Penn Mutual in Wichita, happened to be in the office about a week later. He asked Marilyn, "What's your husband going to do when he gets out of the air force?"

She said, "Well, he wants to sell something. He said something the other night about life insurance."

That night, Marilyn and I had dinner with Paul. He talked to me about the opportunities of the business of insurance, and I was sold at that point.

I certainly had an intellectual philosophy and really believed that it was the right way to go.

Right after I got into the business, I sold a $10,000 term insurance policy to a senior at a state college in Kansas who was a second-string All-American baseball player, a great athlete. He drowned at a fraternity picnic four days after I took the application.

Thank God I could take it nonmedically, and I could bind it. That was my first death claim. It was too soon. Incidentally, the guy's little brother, who was also a great athlete, went on to become a chief actuary for a major life insurance company. He told me many times that the reason he did it was because of the benefits that the $10,000 provided for his parents and helped him get through school.

A Career That Made My Four Wishes Come True

Fate is a funny thing. When I was in the service, I had the opportunity to have a great commanding officer, Gen. Joseph "Smoky" Caldara. For some reason, he took a liking to me, and we had a couple of conversations about the future. He said, "I'm going to give you a book to read." He gave me *Think and Grow Rich* by Napoleon Hill. As I read it, I wrote down and put in my wallet a list of four things I wanted for my future.

> I wrote down and put in my wallet a list of four things I wanted for my future.

The first one was that I could find a job to get when I got out and that I could be in a profession where I could serve people. That's always something I have believed in, like the ministry, but it's true that a lot of people laughed about it because no one would imagine me as a minister. I came pretty close to it. But I realized that I could do something for people that impacted their lives to the degree that we do with our business in financial planning. The financial planning in those days was minor compared to today, but it was just as important.

The second thing I wrote down was that I wanted to be independent. I wanted to be in a business where my income was dependent on what I did, not what a corporation did or what a bureaucracy would provide. Now, remember, this was 1952, and Paul, the agency's top agent, told me that Maury Coulson had earned more than $100,000 the year before (1951). I remember thinking, "Wow, he must be kind of like God."

Paul said, "No, you'll meet him, and you'll realize that that's the opportunity you could have too. You can write your own check in the future."

The third thing is that I wanted to be an entrepreneur and have a high income. That is vital—you have to want to be an entrepreneur. You have to want to be in business for yourself. Now, having grown up on the farm and having run the farm from the time I was about fourteen years old, I was an entrepreneur, and that's what I was seeking.

Fourth, I wanted to be recognized for my achievements. While we were having this conversation that night, Maury Colson and I talked about a lot of stuff, and I talked about playing basketball a little bit. He said, "You like to get the applause and the recognition for playing a good game, don't you?"

I said, "Oh, sure."

"Well, you'll get that in spades in our business if you do well." But then he said, "You've got to realize one thing. You have four reasons you ought to forget the whole darn thing tonight. Number one, you're going to have to put in a lot of hours, just like a doctor does or anyone starting their own business." He said that could be sixty or eighty to a hundred hours a week. "Secondly, you are going to get an awful lot of no's." This was before Al Granum had started the One Card System and gave us a lot of stats. He said, "You want to have at least five hundred clients. To have five hundred clients, you're going to have to call a lot of people, and about twenty thousand people are going to say no. If you're thin-skinned and you can't take no, then forget it. That's the third thing." Then he said, "The last thing is that people are going to look at you and say you're one step above a used-car salesman when you tell them that you're going to sell life insurance."

I thought about the four problems. I knew they were challenges I could overcome because I had already been through some things in life. That's how I came into the business. To me, it was an opportunity, and the only question was whether or not I was man enough to be able to succeed in the business.

Advice to Clients: Secure Life Insurance, and Worry Less

I don't think there's any doubt that the greatest foundation that people should have is the foundation of the Miracle of Life Insurance—especially the foundation of whole life or guaranteed life insurance. I don't really think that's changed any in the sixty-plus years I have been in the business, except that it's more prominent today. I think there have been too many situations where people have not had that foundation.

My wonderful wife, Marilyn, died after fifty-one years, and I later married my second wife, Arlene. Arlene and I are down at our condo in Florida. Our neighbors are very good friends of ours. They were chatting the other day when the stock market was bouncing around and wondering whether or not they were going to be able to stay at the condo. I had been through that with them in 2008 because they are both uninsurable and have been for quite some time. Their 401(k) accounts had been decimated at that point. So now they're worried again, going through the same thing. Had they gotten a good, sound foundation of permanent life insurance, they would have been concerned, but not to the degree they are now.

I have had so many conversations with people in their thirties and forties who have earned a lot of money—doctors, attorneys, business owners—and have gone through particularly tough times. It may not have been based on the economy, but it is based on life. They didn't have the money to take care of some of the things they had to take care of.

> There is no doubt that so many of the deaths and illnesses are caused by the worry that people have about their financial situations.

The other thing that I have seen is you have "sandwich" families—you have someone who has done well, but their parents didn't plan well financially. They haven't planned well financially, either, and they find that their kids are coming out of college and having a tough time getting a job, in some cases. So now they are in a position where they can't make the choices they would perhaps like to make. When people have a good, solid financial plan and a good, solid financial planner working with them, getting them to do the right things at the right time, they place themselves in a position to also accomplish something else. My daughter, Rhonda, is a doctor, and she sends me information about medical associations. There is no doubt that so many of the deaths and illnesses are caused by the worry that people have about their financial situations. I really feel that if you have a good financial planner and the right products, and if you are doing the right things, your health situation is going to be substantially better. If consumers want to build wholesome lives, if they want to be able to take care of the eventualities, they have to have a good, sound financial plan.

Advice to Agents and Advisors: Return to the Basics—Life Insurance

When you go to a cocktail party, people aren't going to talk about their life insurance or their stocks and bonds, or the fact that they made a lot or didn't do well. This is not a sexy business to be in. It's a solid business, it's a wonderful business, and it's something that's vitally important. People coming into the business today and those who are in the business must recognize that the very foundation that they should have begins with life insurance, then disability insurance, and then conservative investments. Then if they want to shoot craps after that, they can.

I have spoken to our own company about the financial planning, the Miracle of Life Insurance. It's not in opposition to annuities or investments; it's just a simple fact of life. I have sat through company meetings, and the Miracle of Life Insurance is seldom discussed at any great length. People are very enamored with annuities and with investments.

And I think we have got to get back to the fundamentals of financial planning and the Miracle of Life Insurance and understand that it's absolutely vital; it's not just a nice thing to have.

The home offices have to get on track. I was in an agency of another company, speaking to their group, and 70 percent of their income is coming from annuities and investment income, managed funds. It is sad because in a good marketplace, you can't tell me that their clients don't need more life insurance. I got into a very serious conversation with a couple of top producers. They had to admit in the past three years, some of their clients have died without having enough life insurance, and the annuities and investments basically did not bail them out. So I just think that we have got to get back and preach the Miracle of Life Insurance where it's needed and teach people how to use it effectively.

It's Human Nature to Pick the Low-Hanging Fruit and Avoid Tough Conversations

God has built us in a way that our human nature is to pick the low-hanging fruit, so to speak, and take the easy way. We all know that when we're doing financial planning and life insurance is a measured part of the solution, we have to do all the applications and all the compliance, get the examinations done, and get the statements in. But from the time an agent gives a client the life insurance application to the time it gets issued is substantially longer than if the client rolls over a 401(k) plan.

Secondly, people just don't like, and never have liked, to talk about dying too soon. It's not a pleasant conversation to have. But it's something that ministers, priests, and rabbis talk about all the time. We need to make certain that our prospects and our clients are able to deal with the realities of life. We emphasize so much the fact that people are living longer, and I'm certainly an example of that. But the fact also remains that many people do not. Arlene's daughter, Carol, is dying of ALS at age fifty-seven. We have all seen so many young people die at the younger ages, in their twenties, thirties, and forties. We have got to get people away from picking the low-hanging fruit and looking for the easy way out.

The last thing is this—harkening back to the fact that people don't like to talk about it. Most agents don't like to force—I call it "force" because I really think it is—they force their clients to really look at premature death and disability. It's a tough conversation. But if they're going to be professional, they're going to have to discuss both death and disability.

You have to be willing to *irritate* your prospect to do the right things and think about the right things. If you're not willing to get them irritated to do the right things, then you're probably in the wrong business.

General Agents Are My Hope for the Future

The people I think can make the difference and create the future that our business should have are the General Agents—those who are recruiting, teaching, training, and advising the people in our business every day of their lives. I think The American College will be a big factor in building the future of this business.

GAMA's annual LAMP conference is a big pivot point because it's the one session that we can all go to each year and continue to have our philosophy backed up by so many great people. But I don't see that it's going to come from any other place. I have had to wrestle with the Department of Labor regarding this mess they're trying to run through [with enacting a fiduciary standard]. Your government is not going to do a darn thing to help you. They are going to do almost everything they possibly can to hurt us and keep us from doing what's right for our clients. So the future of the industry lies in the hands of people like you.

One of the things I worry about is that we, as a society, have found ourselves wandering away from doing the right thing in a lot of different areas. Whether you're talking about being a parent, a financial planner, a doctor, or the clergy, I think that, as a society, we are wandering away from the realities of what life should be about.

> I think we've got to penetrate the middle-income market effectively and do what's right for them.

Penn Mutual had a darn good year last year, with around 30 percent-plus in life premiums, what they call a life-weighted premium. But we find ourselves elephant hunting, cherry picking, whatever you want to call it. So a good portion of our business last year came from large cases, $5 million, $10 million, $20 million cases, large premiums. A lot of it was through premium finance. I think we've got to penetrate the middle-income market effectively and do what's right for them.

This is a wonderful business. You know, after sixty-plus years, I wouldn't have chosen anything else. It's a fantastic business to be in, and we need to be out there preaching the Miracle of Life Insurance every day.

CHAPTER 31

EMILY VINER

Vice President of Agency Growth and Development

The Guardian Life Insurance Company of America

Greater New York City Area

Emily joined Guardian in 1998 after starting her career in the field. An advocate for the career and a mentor to many, Emily has a purpose and passion for securing the future of advisor distribution and leaving a legacy of gender-balanced leadership.

She is responsible for the growth, development, and retention of Guardian's Leadership Bench, in addition to heading Guardian's strategy to create gender, ethnic, and generational diversity in its advisor ranks.

A frequent speaker at industry events, Emily has also published numerous articles in insurance industry publications on the topics of recruiting, coaching, and developing tomorrow's leaders. She was a main-platform speaker at LAMP 2016, presenting groundbreaking research on the topic of closing the gender gap in sales.

Emily was the 2015 recipient of GAMA International's Cy Pick Award. In 2009, she was named the Women in Insurance and Financial Services (WIFS) Woman of the Year.

EMILY'S STORY

Getting the Chills Told Me I Was Embarking on the Right Career

I graduated from college with a degree in marketing and economics. When I went in for my first interview for a marketing job, I found myself being seated at a typewriter. I asked, "What's this?"

They said, "We need to test your typing skills."

I was wondering "For what?" when they said, "Don't worry. Just do it."

I had thought that when I went for a marketing position, I would be a marketer, not a secretary. I sat there and thought, "You know, I'm the first kid in my family to go to college. Is this what I have worked so hard for, putting myself through college waitressing? Is this all there is?"

Although I took the typing test, I never took the job, of course. And then I went into sales in another industry—I was a search consultant in the banking industry in the mid-1980s. By the late 1980s, banking was falling apart in the Northeast...we had yet to realize the global economy! I was kind of hooked on sales at that point, but there was no meaning in the sales I was doing; there was no connection. In 1989, I saw an ad for sales in financial services, and like many ads, it was vague, so I had no idea what it was all about. I found out that it was for a life insurance agent position. I thought, "What's life insurance?" During the selection process, I realized I could sell something that changes people's lives and could have changed mine.

All of a sudden, I got chills...when I was in high school, my father died suddenly of a heart attack at age forty-eight, when my mother was just forty-two years old. Although there was a little bit of cash under the mattress, there was no planning done, and there was certainly no life insurance.

My mother was a hard-working seamstress, and my father had been a hard-working house painter. My brother and I are first-generation Americans.

So at that moment when I learned what life insurance is, I realized, "Oh, my gosh, if my mom had life insurance...if my dad had had it, everything would be different." I didn't even know the differences between term and whole life, but it didn't matter. I just knew that this was something that my parents should have had and that other people should have. So at age twenty-eight, I went into the interview with my Rolodex full of contacts, and I was psyched. I knew I had found what I was supposed to do. I was so excited, and they were really excited!

It was a startup general agency for MassMutual in Connecticut, and it was a lot of fun. I was there from 1989 to 1996 and quickly went into recruiting and management development. In 1995, I spoke at LAMP because we had gone from the bottom of MassMutual to number ten in new manpower development. Speaking at LAMP really changed the direction of my career...I was offered the opportunity to get into a corporate space and realized I could influence the career-distribution system at a national level at Guardian. I could impact even more people and more families across the country.

I was really fortunate as a young woman to find such purpose and passion early in my life. But sometimes it was really difficult, and there were moments when I thought, "I don't know why I'm doing this." You know, as a manager, you find eight great people you think are going to start with the firm, and only one shows up. I often wondered, "Do I want it more than they do?" But it was so rewarding to sit down with clients and see the relief people had when we helped them make a decision. We have to be advocates, and the advocate role was so powerful for me. Even today when I am the client sitting down with my agent, it gives me a good feeling. Early on, I saw the "lightbulb" go on when people realized the value of life insurance. They would say, "Oh! I see what this could mean for my family."

That positive feeling has never left me, that realization that we are impacting people's lives. I see it when we run programs for new advisors. I can see the ones in the audience or group who haven't crossed the bridge yet. They haven't dedicated themselves yet because they're still not sure, and it's still so hard. We have to give them stories to borrow. It is kind of an advocacy effort. If you don't have that personal story yet, then the impact of life insurance doesn't have as much meaning.

> If you don't have that personal story yet, then the impact of life insurance doesn't have as much meaning.

About three years ago, I bought another whole life insurance policy, and I still get such a good feeling because I know what I'm doing. That's for my husband and me for our retirement and for our children after we are gone, because life insurance will always be there. No matter what we do as far as spending down our assets, my estate will be replenished. That is the type of thing I didn't understand when I walked into that office with that Rolodex in 1989, but today it makes such a difference. It has offered so much to my family and me, and to my mom. She just turned eighty and is doing great. I am able to help her along the way financially because of what this business has done for me.

Advice for Consumers: Find an Advisor You Would Invite to Dinner

Gather the right information for yourself, find the right advisor, and listen to your advisor's recommendations. There is so much hype, and I get really frustrated with some of the misinformation that the media and some personalities on TV or social media put out there. They're not always 100 percent accurate. There's never one way to plan the future for every single person. Advisors are educated and trained to find the right solution for each client.

My advice is just to make sure that you always have life insurance as the foundation of your financial plan, that you understand protection first, and that you understand what "human life value" means. Understand the idea that insurance companies are not going to try to sell you more life insurance than you need because if they did that, they wouldn't be in business.

I'm an advocate of whole life insurance, but of course there are many differing views and many different products that fit different situations. Do your homework, and find an advisor you trust. Find someone you really feel comfortable with, someone you would spend time with outside of the financial planning process—just as we look at a potential advisor. Would you spend time with them? Would you invite them to your home for dinner? That should be how you feel about your advisor.

Advice for Agents and Advisors: Find a Great Mentor

I think the key for people coming into this career is to find a mentor. There are always great managers, great leaders, and great training programs. But to be able to come in as a protégé and to have someone you can really learn the fundamentals from, someone you can lean on, is important. I really believe the days of the lone-wolf advisor are beyond us. It takes a village. Find the village you want to live in for a long time. It has to support you.

Do your homework…just like we tell our clients. Do your due diligence on the people in the firm and what they're going to offer. Determine what you can offer and what your part of the equation is. What are you bringing to the table? What's the firm bringing to the table? What is the mentor or manager bringing to the table? Can that help you be an active and supportive member of that village? That's really the important thing.

Our Future Depends on Generational, Ethnic, and Gender Diversity

My hope is that fifty years from now, advisor distribution will be strong and relevant… that people will still be helping other people do the things they have to do to have a solid financial foundation.

Our advisor population is aging. That's why we need to focus on generational diversity. We have to bring younger people into the business. What's nice is that at Guardian, we're encouraging our senior advisors who are top producers to transition what they know to the next generation. So I'm excited about that, and we're excited to see that in our company.

> **We have to bring younger people into the business.**

We need to really look at gender, ethnic, and generational diversity. We still have a long way to go, and I think we have to become advocates for sales as an industry. The problem is bigger than us. The problem is that many people—women in particular—aren't sold on sales, so we have to become advocates. It is similar to the initiative we saw in our schools ten or fifteen years ago around STEM [science, technology, engineering, and math]. Yes, I am comparing STEM to sales because this career requires skill and aptitude, and it's such an amazing career for the right person. Many people don't understand or realize what it means to be in sales, to be an entrepreneur, and how you can help guide people on a journey. We must help people understand what sales is and means when connected to purpose and passion.

So we have to break down the stereotypes. My hope is that we can bring in a whole new generation of very diverse people who are diverse in thinking and diverse in where they are from. They can help people across the country in every community find an advisor within a firm whom they feel comfortable with.

183

CHAPTER 32

HOW FORTUNATE WE ARE THAT LIFE INSURANCE DOES EXIST

Blessings
Remember to count them
each and every day

In the introduction to this book, we asked you to imagine if life insurance didn't exist. Now that you know more about the Miracle of Life Insurance, you know how fortunate we all are that it does exist. Upon the death of an income earner who has life insurance in place, a financial advisor delivers a check to the beneficiaries, keeping the promise that was made the moment the life insurance policy went into effect. No other product does that.

TAKE ADVANTAGE OF THIS MIRACULOUS PRODUCT

Our hope is that you will take advantage of this miraculous product. If you are a financial advisor, we hope you now have a greater appreciation of this true miracle when you interact with clients. And if you are a primary income earner in your family, we hope you have a greater understanding and appreciation of life insurance. We hope you are a person of character who will provide your family with one of the greatest gifts available—financial security for the future. Purchasing the proper amount of life insurance *shows* your family that you love them beyond your physical years.

For the last chapter of this book, we thought it would be appropriate to include one of the last chapters ("Get Rich Quick: Count Your Blessings") of Ed's 2013 book, *Be the First Believer*.[9] It emphasizes the importance of being a grateful person, of appreciating all the wonderful blessings and opportunities in our lives. With those blessings come responsibility, obligation, and commitment.

> If there's one thing you can do in your lifetime to demonstrate that gratitude, it is to be responsible for what you are grateful for. If you are truly grateful for those relationships, you will take responsibility for them. The greatest way to do that is through the Miracle of Life Insurance.

The exercise below will guide you in identifying all the reasons you want to own the proper amount of life insurance and secure the future for the people you truly are blessed to have in your life.

GET RICH QUICK: COUNT YOUR BLESSINGS

We have a tendency to often focus on the few things we don't have in our lives at the expense or mistake of overlooking or neglecting *all* of the wonderful blessings we do have and enjoy on almost a constant basis. We forget that most of the precious gifts we have in life have been freely given to us. We have our health, our ability to think, to love, to walk, run, laugh, cry, forgive, breathe, see, hear, touch, taste—the list goes on and on and on. We overlook the loving relationships we have, the fact that we have opportunities, a school we attend, a team we play on, or a company we work for or lead.

> We forget that most of the precious gifts we have in life have been freely given to us.

---

9. Ed Deutschlander and Rich Campe, *Be the First Believer* (Minneapolis: Bethany Press International, 2013), 162–4.

An exercise I learned a long time ago is to take a few moments in a quiet place with a pad of paper and a pen and to begin to list all the gifts, blessings, and things we are thankful and grateful for in our lives. It doesn't take long for us to see that that list far outweighs the few items we do not have or the few inconveniences we are experiencing at the moment. This exercise brings perspective and quickly has the impact it is intended to have: to allow us to understand that we are indeed *rich*. There really is only one true way to get rich quick, and that is to take inventory of all the good that is going on in our lives and to count our blessings.

Years ago, I came across a "quiz" that I have found extremely helpful in maintaining the right perspective, having an attitude of gratitude, and keeping with the "spirit" of counting my blessings:

1. Name the five wealthiest people in the world.

2. Name ten people who have won the Nobel or Pulitzer Prize.

3. Name the last five winners of the Miss America contest.

4. Name the last five Heisman Trophy winners.

5. Name the last half dozen Academy Award winners for best actor.

6. Name the last decade's worth of World Series winners.

How did you do?

The point is that we don't remember the headliners of yesterday, even though these are no second-rate achievers. They are the best in their fields. They are the people our society puts on a pedestal. These are the rich, the smart, the beautiful, and the athletic. But the applause dies. Awards tarnish. Achievements are forgotten. Accolades and certificates are buried with their owners.

Here is another quiz. See if you fare better with this one:

1. List a few teachers who aided your journey through school.

2. Name three friends who have helped you through a difficult time.

3. Name five people who have taught you something worthwhile.

4. Think of a few people who have made you feel appreciated and special.

5. Think of five people you enjoy spending time with.

6. Name half a dozen heroes whose stories have inspired you.

Chances are you did much better this time, and the reason is this:

The people who make a difference in your life are not the ones with the most credentials, the most money, or the most awards.

They are the ones who care.

I encourage you to take a few moments now and think of the wonderful relationships you have in your life. For that matter, write out the following statement on a piece of paper:

I cannot imagine my life without: _____

_____

_____

_____

_____

Take a few minutes and let your mind wander. Begin writing down the names of everyone you feel has had an impact, to some degree, in your life. Also begin writing down the organizations, institutions, places, and events that complete the sentence above.

These, my friends, are the blessings, people, places, moments, and experiences that enrich our lives. Cherish these and nurture them, as they will constantly bring you a sense of peacefulness and joy.

The Miracle of Life insurance is the most powerful way to demonstrate responsibility for those who mean the most to us.

CHAPTER 33

ABOUT THE AUTHORS

Edward G. Deutschlander, CLU®, CLF®

Chief Executive Officer, North Star Resource Group

612-617-6103

ed@northstarfinancial.com

Ed Deutschlander currently serves as CEO at North Star Resource Group. Ed became only the second CEO in North Star's history on January 1, 2016. North Star has more than $6 billion of client assets entrusted to it, and its origins trace back to 1908 in the Twin Cities community.

Ed started at North Star Resource Group in 1993 immediately upon graduation from Macalester College. His career path has been as a Financial Advisor (1993-94), Recruiter (1995-96), National Recruiting Director (1997-99), Vice President (2000-03), Executive Vice President (2004-2007), President (2008-11) and CEO-Elect (2012-15).

GAMA International[1] ranks North Star Resource Group as the largest privately held independent financial firm in the industry. With Ed's leadership and guidance, North Star received the following prestigious honors in 2015-16:

- Finalist for the Invest in Others Corporate Philanthropy Award (2015 and 2016)

- Top Workplaces in Minnesota, *Star Tribune* (2016)

- Best in Class: Midsize Company, *Minnesota Business Magazine*'s Community Impact Awards (2016)

- Better Business Bureau's Torch Awards for Ethics[3] (2015-16)

- Minnesota Business Ethics Award (2015)

- 100 Best Companies to Work For (2015)

- *INC.* Magazine's Top 5,000 Fastest-Growing Private Companies in the Nation (2015)

- Master Firm Award, GAMA International (2015)[1]

In 2002, Ed became the youngest Managing Partner nationally for the Securian Network, which has more than thirty advising firms throughout the country.

Ed is a past president of GAMA International (2007-08),[1] which serves the professional development needs of individuals and companies engaged in the ethical distribution of financial services and products. GAMA International has approximately 10,000 members who are responsible for more than 100,000 financial advisors who serve more than 40 million clients. Ed was asked to serve on the Board of Directors in 2001 at the age of 29 and became the youngest board member and president in GAMA's 50-plus-year history. He has also been published in numerous publications whose topics include recruiting, leadership selection, training, and development of financial advisors.

In addition, Ed is frequently and heavily quoted throughout the financial services industry, and he is recognized as one of the premier recruiters in the financial services industry. His "Recruiter's Creed" is often used and cited at industry meetings and events. He also is the creator of "Do Well by Doing Good." These two products have educated and been used by thousands of financial services leaders. Since 1998, when he was 27, Ed has been hired as a consultant by many of the largest insurance companies in the world to help them better their recruitment, training, and leadership development programs. Ed has been asked to present internationally in China, Thailand, Singapore, Hong Kong, Mexico, Malaysia, the Philippines, South America, Greece, and Canada and has educated tens of thousands of managers and advisors in the financial services industry by giving several hundred professional presentations. North Star's training program is featured in two *New York Times* Best Sellers, *What the Dog Saw* by Malcolm Gladwell and *Use Your Head to Get Your Foot in the Door* by Harvey Mackay.

Ed is a published author of two other books; *Be the First Believer* and *Practice on Purpose.*

Ed was the first recipient of the North Star Resource Group's Medal of Honor, which recognizes servant leadership, selflessness, service, and integrity. He was recognized as Minnesota Life Insurance Company's Recruiter of the Year every year he was eligible. Since then, under his guidance and tutelage, he has trained two recipients of that prestigious award. Ed has been a keynote speaker at the annual meetings of GAMA International[1] and LIMRA (Life Insurance Marketing and Research Association), and he has addressed groups at the annual meetings of MDRT (Million Dollar Round Table)[3] and NAIFA (National Association of Insurance and Financial Advisors).[2]

He has won numerous management awards from GAMA International and in 2002 was the only person in the industry of the 5,000 members eligible to receive the Career Development Award, Platinum level. Ed holds the CLU (Chartered Life Underwriter) and CLF (Chartered Leadership Fellow) designations and was at the time the youngest person to achieve the CLF designation awarded by The American College. In 2008, NAIFA recognized Ed as one of the "4 under 40" award winners for his career accomplishments.[2] In 2010, the *Minneapolis/St. Paul Business Journal* named him as one of its "40 under 40" award winners.[3]

In 2013, Ed served on the Board of Trustees for NAIFA, which has more than 40,000 members nationally. He was asked to serve a second one-year term in 2014. He currently serves on the Board of Trustees Executive Committee and Finance Committee for the GAMA International Foundation.

COMMUNITY INVOLVEMENT

In 2004, Ed was asked to serve as one of the founding board members of the Scott Richards North Star Charitable Foundation (SRNSCF). North Star created this foundation and donates 10 percent of its profits annually. Since the foundation's inception, North Star has donated more than $3 million to charities in the past ten years. The SRNSCF donates annually to the following charities; breast cancer, ataxia, cystic fibrosis, Alzheimer's disease, and myeofibrosis.

Ed and his wife, Toni, founded and championed the Twin Cities Bikes for Kids program in 2004. Bikes for Kids makes it possible for disadvantaged youth to receive a brand-new bike at a surprise holiday party hosted annually at the Twin Cities. In the past twelve years, more than 4,000 children in the Big Brothers/Big Sisters Greater Twin Cities program have received this holiday gift and surprise.

PERSONAL

Ed is a 1993 graduate of Macalester College in St. Paul, Minnesota, where he played, started, and lettered in two varsity sports (football and baseball) and served as captain of his college football team.

In addition to his professional and industry commitments, Ed enjoys speaking to and educating today's college students. He is asked to speak at universities and colleges around the country on the topic of life after college. He shares lessons on leadership and personal development to assist them in their life endeavors after college.

Ed resides in Carver, Minnesota, with his wife of 25 years, Toni, and their four children: Ashley, Jacob, Hannah, and William.

---

1 **GAMA International** is a membership organization for which individuals must submit applications and payment. The organization is geared toward those in a recruiting, training, or supervision role in the financial services industry. Awards are based primarily on commissions, premiums, or fees generated from investment and insurance products and other criteria relative to leadership, achievement, and recruiting selected by the applicant. Individuals must be current with membership dues and submit an application fee for consideration. Working with this individual is not a guarantee of future financial results. Investors should conduct their own evaluation.

2 **NAIFA, Securian, and Firm Awards:** Awards and club membership are based primarily on commissions, premiums, or fees generated from investment and insurance products and other criteria relative to leadership and achievement. Working with this individual or firm is not a guarantee of future financial results. Investors should conduct their own evaluation.

3 **Million Dollar Round Table (MDRT)** is an independent membership organization of life insurance and financial service professionals. Membership levels are based on commissions, premiums, or fees generated within a year from investment and insurance products. Members must apply annually and pay a fee. Members must be members in good standing of a Professional Association that has met the following criteria: must have been in existence at least two years, must have one hundred or more members, must be a nonprofit organization, and must have a code of ethics and an effective means of dealing with breaches of its code. Members must also adhere to the MDRT Code of Ethics. Working with this advisor is not a guarantee of future financial results. Investors should conduct their own evaluation.

P. Shaun McDuffee, CLU®, ChFC®, AEP®, CEPA®

Senior Vice President, North Star Resource Group

512-610-4050

Shaun.McDuffee@northstarfinancial.com

Shaun McDuffee is a Senior Vice President at North Star Resource Group and is one of seven officers responsible for shaping the company's direction. With the help of Shaun's leadership, North Star has become one of the largest independent financial services firms in the world.

Shaun is one of the original founders of North Star's Medical Division. He has specialized in assisting physicians and their families since 1990, and his guidance has been critical in helping thousands of physicians overcome the financial challenges unique to their career.

Every year since 1998, Shaun has been distinguished by the Million Dollar Round Table (MDRT), The Premier Association of Financial Professionals®, which recognizes financial advisors worldwide. He also has been a member of the MDRT's prestigious Top of the Table every year since 2003 Shaun was a featured main-platform speaker at the 2005 GAMA International conference, and he has been a break-out-session speaker at MDRT, LAMP, and the MDRT International Conference, where he spoke about the importance of mentoring.

He has received the NAIFA Quality Award (NQA) for Client Service every year since 1997, and he was only the third person to receive the prestigious Samuel R. Weems Award, presented in recognition of his many contributions to the industry and to the International Million Dollar Round Table.

Shaun and his wife, Kristin, founded Stop Alzheimer's Now (SAN) in 2013. SAN is a 501(c)(3) nonprofit, dedicated to raising awareness and funding for Alzheimer's research. He and Kristin founded the McDuffee Family Foundation in 2006 to aid children's causes in the communities they have lived in. Shaun also serves on the board of the North Star Charitable Foundation.

Consistently recognized as one of North Star's top-producing financial advisors, Shaun has finished in the top five nationwide since 1998. He has been recognized as North Star's top advisor nationally every year since 2003. In addition, he was recognized as Securian's Diamond (top) Advisor nationally in 2006, 2009, and 2011. He was recognized as Securian's Gold (runner-up) Advisor of the Year in 2004, 2005, 2007, 2010, 2012, and 2015.

Shaun's division has become a consistent front-runner within the firm for death benefits (DB) in force (as of 9/30/16), a feat he and his team accomplished in only six

and a half years. His division currently has $4.2 billion in total DB in force. Shaun's goal is to place $1.5 billion of protection for his clients' families in 2016. He projects that in the next three to four years, his division will be the second-largest firm within the Securian system based on DB placed and in force. At a time when many people are walking by the protection element of the financial plan, we are standing strong to help ensure that our clients' families are out of harm's way in the event of tragedy.

Shaun is a 1990 graduate of the University of Wisconsin–Madison. He enjoys his life as the only male in his house, in Austin, Texas, being hopelessly outnumbered by his wife Kristin; daughters Sophie, Ingrid, and Annabel; and their dogs, Molly and Maggie!

Shaun is the founder and president of the foundation called Stop Alzheimer's Now.

Phillip C. Richards, CFP®, CLU®, RHU®

Founder and Executive Chairman,
North Star Resource Group

612-617-6167

phil.richards@northstarfinancial.com

Phillip C. Richards, CFP®, CLU, RHU is the Founder and Executive Chairman of the affiliated companies that comprise North Star Resource Group. North Star represents a fully integrated array of financial services and products for individuals and businesses of all sizes and has over 120,000 clients with offices in 22 states and client assets under management exceeding $6 billion (as of 12/31/15).

Phil received his BS degree in 1962 from Temple University, where he served as Student Body President and received the prestigious Sword Award as outstanding senior classman. A recipient of a four-year wrestling scholarship, he served as team captain and was inducted into the National Wrestling Hall of Fame in 2010 and the National High School Coaches Hall of Fame in 2010. Phil was elected to the Temple University Board of Trustees in 2009 and was the 2016 commencement speaker for Temple University, in the same ceremony in which he was awarded an honorary Doctor of Humane Letters degree. Also in 2016, Phil was inducted into The American College Hall of Fame.

Phil began his professional career in the insurance industry in 1962 with the Penn Mutual Life Insurance Company in Philadelphia. In 1965, he joined Hartford Life, where he led the company in brokerage sales. In 1969, Phil acquired North Star Resource Group, which is celebrating more than 108 years in business, has received the prestigious Master Firm Award from GAMA International[1] every year since 1988. North Star was awarded the Community Service Award from *InvestmentNews* in 2010 and the Better Business Bureau's Integrity Award in 2011 and again in 2016[2]. It was voted one of 100 Best Places to Work in Minnesota in 2015 and received the Minnesota Business Ethics Award in 2015 as well.

A winner of numerous industry awards, Phil is the 2005 Inductee into the GAMA International Hall of Fame and is the only firm leader in the world to have received the International Management Award from GAMA International each and every year (forty-three years) since the inception of that award.[1] In 2007, Phil was named recipient of the 66th annual John Newton Russell Memorial Award, the highest honor in the insurance industry, by The National Association of Insurance and Financial Advisors.[2] Phil's first book, *25 Secrets for Sustainable Success*, was published in March 2007. He co-wrote his second book, *The Sky Is Not the Limit*, in 2014, and *Practice on Purpose* in 2015.

North Star has been the leading outlet for its largest partner, Minnesota Life, for the past twenty-five years. GAMA International has ranked North Star as one of the three

largest organizations of its kind in the world for the past five years.[1] The firm has more than three hundred associates in the firm. Combined Gross Revenues were in excess of $58 million.

Phil is an Adjunct Professor Emeritus for the Carlson School of Management at the University of Minnesota and is a former Adjunct Professor at Central University of Finance and Economics in Beijing. China. He is a four-time chairman of Securian's National Advisory Board and was inducted as its nineteenth Hall of Fame member.[2] He currently serves on the Board of Trustees for The American College in Philadelphia and was inducted into its Hall of Fame in November 2016 in NYC. He serves on the Mayo Clinic of Arizona Leadership Council. He served on the Executive Board of Directors for the Minnesota Council for Quality and is a past president of GAMA International (2002–03).

For forty-five years, he has been an arbitrator for the Better Business Bureau. He is a past chairman of the Board of Directors of the Minnesota/North Dakota Better Business Bureau, and he served on the Board of Directors of the Arizona Quality Council. In addition, he is a past chairman of the LIFE Foundation, as well as a past treasurer of the Arizona Heart Foundation's Board of Trustees. He chairs the Scott Richards North Star Charitable Foundation, which annually receives 10 percent of all of North Star's profits and has given more $3 million to charities in the past ten years.

Phil has been a featured speaker in more than fifteen countries on topics including strategic planning, leadership, and alternate distribution systems in the financial services industry in the twenty-first century. He has addressed the annual meetings of more than 150 major companies; was a main-platform speaker at the GAMA International's LAMP Meeting in 1998 and its Canadian counterpart in Toronto in 1999; was a main-platform speaker in Singapore, Taipei, and Manila in August 2000; and was a main-platform speaker at the Asian Pacific Conference in Bangkok (where he cofounded GAMA Thailand) in 2001 and 2010 and in Singapore in 2011 and 2015; Crete, Greece, in 2002; Athens in 2006, 2010, and 2015; Sydney, Australia, in 2005; and Buenos Aires, Argentina, and Shanghai and Beijing, China, numerous times as a lecturer at Beijing University and Shanghai University for Finance and Economics. Phil was a main-platform speaker for Million Dollar Round Table (MDRT)[3] in Vancouver in 2010 and in Ireland in 2012, as well as GAMA LAMP Asia in 2014 and 2016. He was a 2016 Asia LAMP main-platform speaker in Bangkok and was a featured speaker in Vietnam and Singapore in August, and will be once again in Singapore in March 2017.

----

1 **GAMA International** is a membership organization for which individuals must submit applications and payment. The organization is geared toward those in a recruiting, training, or supervision role in the financial services industry. Awards are based primarily on commissions, premiums, or fees generated from investment and insurance products and other criteria relative to leadership, achievement, and recruiting selected by the applicant. Individuals must be current with membership

dues and submit an application fee for consideration. Working with this individual is not a guarantee of future financial results. Investors should conduct their own evaluation.

2 **NAIFA, Securian, and Firm Awards:** Awards and club membership are based primarily on commissions, premiums, or fees generated from investment and insurance products and other criteria relative to leadership and achievement. Working with this individual or firm is not a guarantee of future financial results. Investors should conduct their own evaluation.

3 **Million Dollar Round Table (MDRT)** is an independent membership organization of life insurance and financial service professionals. Membership levels are based on commissions, premiums, or fees generated within a year from investment and insurance products. Members must apply annually and pay a fee. Members must be members in good standing of a Professional Association that has met the following criteria: must have been in existence at least two years, must have one hundred or more members, must be a nonprofit organization, and must have a code of ethics and an effective means of dealing with breaches of its code. Members must also adhere to the MDRT Code of Ethics. Working with this advisor is not a guarantee of future financial results. Investors should conduct their own evaluation.

1556328

DOFU 11-2016